Benjamin Count of Rumford

Experiments to Determine the Force of Fired Gunpowder

Benjamin Count of Rumford

Experiments to Determine the Force of Fired Gunpowder

ISBN/EAN: 9783337184360

Printed in Europe, USA, Canada, Australia, Japan

Cover: Foto ©ninafisch / pixelio.de

More available books at **www.hansebooks.com**

XII. *Experiments to determine the Force of fired Gunpowder.*
By Benjamin *Count of* Rumford, *F. R. S. M. R. I. A.*

Read May 4, 1797.

No human invention of which we have any authentic records, except, perhaps, the art of printing, has produced such important changes in civil society as the invention of gunpowder. Yet, notwithstanding the uses to which this wonderful agent is applied are so extensive, and though its operations are as surprising as they are important, it seems not to have hitherto been examined with that care and perseverance which it deserves. The explosion of gunpowder is certainly one of the most surprising phænomena we are acquainted with, and I am persuaded it would much oftener have been the subject of the investigations of speculative philosophers, as well as of professional men, in this age of inquiry, were it not for the danger attending the experiments : but the force of gunpowder is so great, and its effects so sudden and so terrible, that, notwithstanding all the precautions possible, there is ever a considerable degree of danger attending the management of it, as I have more than once found to my cost.

Several eminent philosophers and mathematicians, it is true, have, from time to time, employed their attention upon this curious subject; and the modern improvements in chemistry have given us a considerable insight into the cause, and the nature of the explosion which takes place in the inflammation of gunpowder; and the nature and properties of the elastic fluids generated in its combustion. But the great desideratum, the real measure of the initial expansive force of inflamed gunpowder, so far from being known, has hitherto been rather guessed at than determined; and no argument can be more convincing to show our total ignorance upon that subject, than the difference in the opinions of the greatest mathematicians of the age, who have undertaken its investigation.

The ingenious Mr. ROBINS, who made a great number of very curious experiments upon gunpowder, and who, I believe, has done more towards perfecting the art of gunnery than any other individual, concluded, as the result of all his inquiries and computations, that the force of the elastic fluid generated in the combustion of gunpowder is 1000 times greater than the mean pressure of the atmosphere. But the celebrated mathematician DANIEL BERNOUILLI determines its force to be not less than 10,000 times that pressure, or ten times greater than Mr. ROBINS made it.

Struck with this great difference in the results of the computations of these two able mathematicians, as well as with the subject itself, which appeared to me to be both curious and important, I many years ago set about making experiments upon gunpowder, with a view principally of determining the point in question, namely, *its initial expansive force* when fired; and I have ever since, occasionally, from time to time, as I have found leisure and convenient opportunities, continued these inquiries.

In a paper printed in the year 1781, in the LXXI. Volume of the Philosophical Transactions, I gave an account of an

experiment (No. 92.) by which it appeared that, calculating
even upon Mr. ROBINS's own principles, the force of gunpowder, instead of being 1000 times, must at least be 1308 times
greater than the mean pressure of the atmosphere. However,
not only that experiment, but many others, mentioned in the
same paper, had given me abundant reason to conclude that the
principles assumed by Mr. ROBINS, in his treatise upon gunnery,
were erroneous; and I saw no possibility of ever being able to
determine the initial force of gunpowder by the methods he had
proposed, and which I had till then followed in my experiments.
Unwilling to abandon a pursuit which had already cost me
much pains, I came to a resolution to strike out a new road,
and to endeavour to ascertain the force of gunpowder by *actual
measurement*, in a direct and decisive experiment.

   I shall not here give a detail of the numerous difficulties and
disappointments I met with in the course of these dangerous
pursuits; it will be sufficient briefly to mention the plan of
operations I formed, in order to obtain the end I proposed, and
to give a cursory view of the train of unsuccessful experiments
by which I was at length led to the discovery of the truly astonishing force of gunpowder;—a force at least *fifty thousand*
times greater than the mean pressure of the atmosphere!

   My first attempts were to fire gunpowder in a confined space,
thinking, that when I had accomplished this, I should find
means, without much difficulty, to measure its elastic force.
To this end, I caused a short gun-barrel to be made, of the
best wrought iron, and of uncommon strength; the diameter
of its bore was $\frac{3}{4}$ of an inch, its length 5 inches, and the thickness of the metal was equal to the diameter of the bore, so that
its external diameter was $2\frac{1}{4}$ inches. It was closed at both

ends, by two long screws, like the breech-pin of a musket; each of which entered 2 inches into the bore, leaving only a vacuity of 1 inch in length for the charge. The powder was introduced into this cavity by taking out one of the screws, or breech-pins; which being afterwards screwed into its place again, and both ends of the barrel closed up, fire was communicated to the powder by a very narrow vent, made in the axis of one of the breech-pins for that purpose. The chamber, which was 1 inch in length, and $\frac{3}{4}$ of an inch in diameter, being about half filled with powder, I expected that when the powder should be fired, the generated elastic fluid being obliged to issue out at so small an opening as the vent, which was no more than $\frac{1}{20}$ of an inch in diameter, instead of giving a smart report, would come out with something like a hissing noise; and I intended, in a future experiment, to confine the generated elastic fluid entirely, by adding a valve to the vent, as I had done in some of my experiments mentioned in my paper published in the LXXI. Volume of the Philosophical Transactions. But when I set fire to the charge (which I took the precaution to do by means of a train), instead of a hissing noise, I was surprised by a very sharp and a very loud report; and, upon examining the barrel, I found the vent augmented to at least four times its former dimensions, and both the screws loosened.

Finding, by the result of this experiment, that I had to do with an agent much more troublesome to manage than I had imagined, I redoubled my precautions. As the barrel was not essentially injured, its ends were now closed up by two new screws, which were firmly fixed in their places by solder, and a new vent was opened in the barrel itself. As both ends of the barrel were now closed up, it was necessary, in order to introduce the powder into the chamber, to make it pass through the vent, or to convey it through some other aperture made for that purpose. The method I employed was as follows: a hole being made in the barrel, about $\frac{1}{10}$ of an inch in diameter, a plug of steel was screwed into this hole; and it was in the centre or axis of the plug that the vent was made. To introduce the powder into the chamber the plug was taken away. The vent was made conical, its largest diameter being inwards, or opening into the chamber; and a conical pin, of hardened steel, was fitted into it; which pin was intended to serve as a valve for closing up the vent, as soon as the powder in the chamber should be inflamed. To give a passage to the fire through the vent in entering the chamber, this pin was pushed a little inwards, so as to leave a small vacuity between its surface and the concave surface of the bore of the vent. But notwithstanding all possible care was taken in the construction of this instrument, to render it perfect in all its parts, the experiment was as unsuccessful as the former: upon firing the powder in the chamber, (though it did not fill more than half its cavity), the generated elastic fluid not only forced its way through the vent, notwithstanding the valve (which appeared not to have had time to close), but it issued with such an astonishing velocity from this small aperture, that instead of coming out with a hissing noise, it gave a report nearly as sharp and as loud as a common musket. Upon examining the vent-plug and the pin, they were both found to be much corroded and damaged; though I had taken the precaution to harden them both before I made the experiment.

I afterwards repeated the experiment with a simple vent,

made very narrow, and lined with gold to prevent its being corroded by the acid vapour generated in the combustion of the gunpowder; but this vent was found, upon trial, to be as little able to withstand the amazing force of the inflamed gunpowder as the others. It was so much, and so irregularly corroded, by the explosion in the first experiment, as to be rendered quite unserviceable; and what is still more extraordinary, the barrel itself, notwithstanding its amazing strength, was blown out into the form of a cask; and though it was cracked, it was not burst quite asunder, nor did it appear that any of the generated elastic fluid had escaped through the crack. The barrel, in the state it was found after this experiment, is still in my possession.

These unsuccessful attempts, and many others of a similar nature, of which it is not necessary to give a particular account, as they all tended to shew that the force of fired gunpowder is in fact much greater than has generally been imagined, instead of discouraging me from pursuing these inquiries, served only to excite my curiosity still more, and to stimulate me to further exertions.

These researches did not by any means appear to me as being merely speculative; on the contrary, I considered the determination of the real force of the elastic fluid generated in the combustion of gunpowder as a matter of great importance.

The use of gunpowder is become so extensive, that very important mechanical improvements can hardly fail to result from any new discoveries relative to its force, and the law of its action. Most of the computations that have hitherto been made relative to the action of gunpowder, have been founded upon the supposition that the elasticity of the generated fluid is as its

H h

density; but if this supposition should prove false, all those computations, with all the practical rules founded on them, must necessarily be erroneous; and the influence of these errors must be as extensive as the uses to which gunpowder is applied.

Having found by experience how difficult it is to confine the elastic vapour generated in the combustion of gunpowder, when the smallest opening is left by which any part of it can escape, it occurred to me, that I might perhaps succeed better by closing up the powder entirely, in such a manner as to leave no opening whatever, by which it could communicate with the external air; and by setting the powder on fire, by causing the heat employed for that purpose to pass through the solid substance of the iron barrel used for confining it. In order to make this experiment, I caused a new barrel to be constructed for that purpose: its length was 3.45 inches, and the diameter of its bore $\frac{7}{10}$ of an inch; its ends were closed up by two screws, each one inch in length, which were firmly and immoveably fixed in their places by solder; a vacuity being left between them in the barrel 1.45 inch in length, which constituted the chamber of the piece; and whose capacity was nearly $\frac{6}{10}$ of a cubic inch. An hole, 0.37 of an inch in diameter, being bored through both sides of the barrel, through the centre of the chamber, and at right angles to its axis, two tubes of iron, 0.37 of an inch in diameter, the diameter of whose bore was $\frac{1}{10}$ of an inch, were firmly fixed in this hole with solder, in such a manner that while their internal openings were exactly opposite to each other, and on opposite sides of the chamber, the axes of their bores were in the same right line. The shortest of these tubes, which projected 1.3 inch beyond the external surface of the barrel, was closed at its projecting end, or rather it was not bored quite through its whole length, $\frac{1}{10}$ of an inch of solid metal being left at its end, which was rounded off in the form of a blunt point. The longer tube, which projected 2.7 inches beyond the surface of the barrel on the other side, and which served for introducing the powder into the chamber, was open; but it could occasionally be closed by a strong screw, furnished with a collar of oiled leather, which was provided for that purpose. The method of making use of this instrument was as follows. The barrel being laid down, or held, in a horizontal position, with the long tube upwards, the charge, which was of the very best fine-grained glazed powder, was poured through this tube into the chamber. In doing this, care must be taken that the cavity of the short tube be completely filled with powder, and this can best be done by pouring in only a small quantity of powder at first, and then, by striking the barrel with a hammer, cause the powder to descend into the short tube. When, by introducing a priming-wire through the long tube, it is found that the short tube is full, it ought to be gently pressed together, or rammed down, by means of the priming-wire, in order to prevent its falling back into the chamber upon moving the barrel out of the horizontal position. The short tube being properly filled, the rest of the charge may be introduced into the chamber, and the end of the long tube closed up by its screw.

More effectually to prevent the elastic fluid generated in the combustion of the charge from finding a passage to escape by this opening, after the charge was introduced into the chamber, the cavity of the long tube was filled up with cold tallow, and the screw that closed up its end (which was $\frac{1}{2}$ an inch long, and but a little more than $\frac{1}{10}$ of an inch in diameter) was pressed down against its leather collar with the utmost force.   The manner of setting fire to the charge was as follows: a block of wrought iron, about $1\frac{1}{2}$ inch square, with a hole in it, capable of receiving nearly the whole of that part of the *short tube* which projects beyond the barrel, being heated red hot, the end of the short tube was introduced into this hole, where it was suffered to remain till the heat, having penetrated the tube, set fire to the powder it contained, and the inflammation was *from thence* communicated to the powder in the chamber.

The result of this experiment fully answered my expectations.   The generated elastic fluid was so completely confined that no part of it could make its escape.   The report of the explosion was so very feeble, as hardly to be audible : indeed it did not by any means deserve the name of a report, and certainly could not have been heard at the distance of twenty paces; it resembled the noise which is occasioned by the breaking of a very small glass tube.

I imagined at first that the powder had not all taken fire, but the heat of the barrel soon convinced me that the explosion must have taken place, and after waiting near half an hour, upon loosening the screw which closed the end of the long vent tube, the confined elastic vapours rushed out with considerable force, and with a noise like that attending the discharge of an air-gun.   The quantity of powder made use of in the experiment was indeed very small, not amounting to

more than $\frac{1}{8}$ part of what the chamber was capable of containing; but having so often had my machinery destroyed in
experiments of this sort, I began now to be more cautious.

Having found means to confine the elastic vapour generated
in the combustion of gunpowder, my next attempts were to
measure its force ; but here again I met with new and almost
insurmountable difficulties. To measure the expansive force
of the vapour, it was necessary to bring it to act upon a
moveable body of known dimensions, and whose resistance to
the efforts of the fluid could be accurately determined; but
this was found to be extremely difficult. I attempted it in
various ways, but without success. I caused a hole to be bored
in the axis of one of the screws, or breech-pins, which closed
up the ends of the barrel just described, and fitting a piston of
hardened steel into this hole (which was $\frac{2}{10}$ of an inch in
diameter), and causing the end of the piston which projected
beyond the end of the barrel to act upon a heavy weight, suspended as a pendulum to a long iron rod, I hoped, by know-
ing the velocity acquired by the weight, from the length of
the arc described by it in its ascent, to be able to calculate the
pressure of the elastic vapour by which it was put in motion ;
but this contrivance was not found to answer, nor did any of
the various alterations and improvements I afterwards made in
the machinery render the results of the experiment at all
satisfactory. It was not only found almost impossible to prevent the escape of the elastic fluid by the sides of the piston,
but the results of apparently similar experiments were so very
different, and so uncertain, that I was often totally at a loss
to account for these extraordinary variations. I was however
at length led to suspect, what I afterwards found abundant

reason to conclude was the real cause of these variations, and of all the principal difficulties which attended the ascertaining the force of fired gunpowder by the methods I had hitherto pursued.

It has generally been believed, after Mr. Robins, that the force of fired gunpowder consists in the action of a permanently elastic fluid, similar in many respects to common atmospheric air; which being generated from the powder in combustion, in great abundance, and being moreover in a very compressed state, and its elasticity being much augmented by the heat (which is likewise generated in the combustion), it escapes with great violence, by every avenue; and produces that loud report, and all those terrible effects, which attend the explosion of gunpowder.

But though this theory is very plausible, and seems upon a cursory view of the subject to account in a satisfactory manner for all the phænomena, yet a more careful examination will shew it to be defective. There is no doubt but the permanently elastic fluids, generated in the combustion of gunpowder, *assist* in producing those effects which result from its explosion; but it will be found, I believe, upon ascertaining the real expansive force of fired gunpowder, that this cause, alone, is quite inadequate to the effects actually produced; and that, therefore, the agency of some other power must necessarily be called in to its assistance.

Mr. Robins has shewn, that if all the permanently elastic fluid generated in the combustion of gunpowder be compressed in the space originally occupied by the powder, and if this fluid so compressed be supposed to be heated to the intense heat of red-hot iron, its elastic force *in that case* will be 1000 times greater than the mean pressure of the atmosphere; and this, according to his theory, is the real measure of the force of gunpowder, *fired in a cavity which it exactly fills.*

But what will become of this theory, and of all the suppositions upon which it is founded, if I shall be able to prove, as I hope to do in the most satisfactory manner, that the force of fired gunpowder, instead of being 1000 times, is at least 50,000 greater than the mean pressure of the atmosphere?

For my part, I know of no way of accounting for this enormous force, but by supposing it to arise principally from the elasticity of the *aqueous vapour* generated from the powder in its combustion. The brilliant discoveries of modern chemists have taught us, that both the constituent parts of which water is composed, and even water itself, exist in the materials which are combined to make gunpowder; and there is much reason to believe that water is actually formed, as well as disengaged, in its combustion. M. LAVOISIER, I know, imagined that the force of fired gunpowder, depends in a great measure upon the expansive force of uncombined *caloric*, supposed to be let loose in great abundance during the combustion or deflagration of the powder: but it is not only dangerous to admit the action of an agent whose existence is not yet clearly demonstrated, but it appears to me that this supposition is quite unnecessary; the elastic force of the heated aqueous vapour, whose existence can hardly be doubted, being quite sufficient to account for all the phænomena. It is well known that the elasticity of aqueous vapour is incomparably more augmented by any given augmentation of temperature, than that of any permanently elastic fluid whatever; and those who are acquainted with the amazing force of steam, when heated only to a few degrees above the boiling point, can easily perceive that its elasticity must be almost infinite when greatly condensed and heated to the temperature of red-hot iron; and this heat it must certainly acquire in the explosion of gunpowder. But if the force of fired gunpowder arises *principally* from the elastic force of heated aqueous vapour, a cannon is nothing more than a *steam-engine* upon a peculiar construction; and upon determining the ratio of the elasticity of this vapour to its density, and to its temperature, a law will be found to obtain, very different from that assumed by Mr. ROBINS, in his Treatise on Gunnery. What this law really is, I do not pretend to have determined with that degree of precision which I wished; but the experiments of which I am about to give an account will, I think, demonstrate in the most satisfactory manner, not only that the force of fired gunpowder is in fact much greater than has been imagined, but also that its force consists principally in the temporary action of a fluid not permanently elastic, and consequently that all the theories hitherto proposed for the elucidation of this subject, must be essentially erroneous.

The first step towards acquiring knowledge is undoubtedly that which leads us to a discovery of the falsehood of received opinions. To a diligent inquirer every common operation, performed in the usual course of practice, is an experiment, from which he endeavours to discover some new fact, or to confirm the result of former inquiries.

Having been engaged many years in the investigation of the force of gunpowder, I occasionally found many opportunities of observing, under a variety of circumstances, the various effects produced by its explosion; and as a long habit of meditating upon this subject rendered every thing relating to it highly interesting to me; I seized these opportunities with avidity, and examined all the various phænomena with steady and indefatigable attention.

During a cruise which I made as a volunteer in the Victory, with the British fleet, under the command of my late worthy friend Sir CHARLES HARDY, in the year 1779, I had many opportunities of attending to the firing of heavy cannon : for though we were not fortunate enough to come to a general action with the enemy, as is well known, yet, as the men were frequently exercised at the great guns, and in firing at marks, and as some of my friends in the fleet, then captains, (since made admirals) as the Honourable KEITH STEWART, who commanded the Berwick of 74 guns—Sir CHARLES DOUGLAS, who commanded the Duke of 98 guns—and Admiral MACBRIDE, who was then captain of the Bienfaisant of 64 guns, were kind enough, at my request, to make a number of experiments, and particularly by firing a greater number of bullets at once from their heavy guns than ever had been done before, and observing the distances at which they fell in the sea ; I had opportunities of making several very interesting observations, which gave me much new light relative to the action of fired gunpowder. And afterwards, when I went out to America, to command a regiment of cavalry which I had raised in that country for the King's service, his Majesty having been graciously pleased to permit me to take out with me from England four pieces of light artillery, constructed under the direction of the late Lieutenant General DESAGULIERS, with a large proportion of ammunition, I made a great number of interesting experiments with these guns, and also with the

ship guns on board the ships of war in which I made my passage to and from America.

It would take up too much time, and draw out this paper
to too great a length, to give an account in detail of all these
experiments, and of the various observations I have had opportunities of making from time to time, relative to this subject.
I shall, therefore, only observe at present, that the result of all
my inquiries tended to confirm me more and more in the
opinion, that the theory generally adopted relative to the explosion of gunpowder was extremely erroneous, and that its
force is in fact much greater than is generally imagined. That
the position of Mr. ROBINS, which supposes the inflammation
and combustion of gunpowder to be so instantaneous " that
" the whole of the charge of a piece of ordnance is actually
" inflamed and converted into an elastic vapour before the
" bullet is sensibly moved from its place," is very far from
being true; and that the ratio of the elasticity of the generated
fluid, to its density, or to the space it occupies as it expands,
is very different from that assumed by Mr. ROBINS.

The rules laid down by Mr. ROBINS for computing the velocities of bullets from their weight, the known dimensions of
the gun, and the quantities of powder made use of for the
charge, may, and certainly do, very often give the velocities
very near the truth; but this is no proof that the principles
upon which these computations are made are just; for it may
easily happen, that a complication of erroneous suppositions
may be so balanced, that the result of a calculation founded
on them may, nevertheless, be very near the truth; and this
is never so likely to happen as when, from known effects, the

action of the powers which produce them are computed. For it is not in general very difficult to assume such principles as, when taken together, may in the most common known cases answer completely all the conditions required. But in such cases, if the truth be discovered with regard to any one of the assumed principles, and it be substituted in the place of the erroneous supposition, the fallacy of the whole hypothesis will immediately become evident.

As I have mentioned the experiments made with heavy artillery, as having been led by their results to form important conjectures relative to the nature of the expansion of the fluid generated in the combustion of gunpowder; it may perhaps be asked, and indeed with some appearance of reason, what the circumstances were which attended the experiments in question, which could justify so important a conclusion as that of the fallacy of the commonly received theory relative to that subject. To this I answer briefly, that in regard to the supposed instantaneous inflammation of the powder, upon which the whole fabric of this theory is built, or rather of all the computations which are grounded upon it, a careful attention to the phænomena which take place upon firing off cannon, led me to suspect, or rather confirmed me in my former suspicions, that however rapid the inflammation of gunpowder may be, its *total combustion* is by no means so sudden as this theory supposes. When a heavy cannon is fired in the common way, that is, when the vent is filled with loose powder, and the piece is fired off with a match, the time employed in the passage of the inflammation through the vent into the chamber of the piece is perfectly sensible, and this time is evidently shorter after the piece has been heated by

repeated firing.   With the same charge, the recoil of a gun,
(and consequently the velocity of its bullet), is greater after
the gun has been heated by repeated firing than when it is cold.
The velocity of the bullet is considerably greater when the cannon is fired off with a vent tube, or by firing a pistol charged
with powder into the open vent, than when the vent is filled
with loose powder.   The velocity of two, three, or more fit
bullets discharged at once from a piece of ordnance, compared
to the velocity of one single bullet discharged by the same
quantity of powder, from the same cannon, is greater than it
ought to be according to the theory.   Considerable quantities
of powder are frequently driven out of cannon and other fire-
arms *unconsumed.*   The manner in which the smoke of gunpowder rises in the air, and is gradually dissolved and rendered
invisible, shews it to partake of the nature of steam.   But not
to take up too much time with these general observations, I
shall proceed to give an account of experiments the results of
which will be considered as more conclusive.

Having found it impossible to measure the elastic force of
fired gunpowder with any degree of precision by any of the
methods before mentioned, I totally changed my plan of operations, and instead of endeavouring to determine its force by
causing the generated elastic fluid to act upon a moveable body
through a determined space, I set about contriving an apparatus in which this fluid should be made to act, by a determined
surface, against a weight, which by being increased at pleasure
should at last be such as would just be able to confine it, and
which in that case would just counterbalance and consequently
measure its elastic force.

The idea of this method of determining the force of fired

gunpowder occurred to me many years ago; but a very expen-
sive and troublesome apparatus being necessary in order to put
it in execution, it was not till the year 1792, when, being
charged with the arrangement of the army of his most Serene
Highness the ELECTOR PALATINE, reigning Duke of Bavaria,
and having all the resources of the military arsenal, and a number of very ingenious workmen at my command, with the per-
mission and approbation of his most Serene Electoral Highness, I set about making the experiments which I shall now
describe: and as they are not only important in themselves,
and in their results, but as they are, I believe, the first of the
kind that have been made, I shall be very particular in my account of them, and of the apparatus used in making them.

One difficulty being got over, that of setting fire to the powder without any communication with the external air, by causing the heat employed for that purpose to pass through the
solid substance of the barrel, it only remained to apply such a
weight to an opening made in the barrel as the whole force of
the generated elastic fluid should not be able to lift, or displace;
but in doing this many precautions were necessary. For, first,
as the force of gunpowder is so very great, it was necessary
to employ an enormous weight to confine it; for, though by
diminishing the size of the opening, the weight would be les-
sened in the same proportion, yet it was necessary to make
this opening of a certain size, otherwise the experiments would
not have been satisfactory; and it was necessary to make the
support or base upon which the barrel was placed very massy
and solid, to prevent the errors which would unavoidably have
arisen from its want of solidity, or from its elasticity.

The annexed drawings (Tab. V.) will give a complete idea

of the whole apparatus made use of in these experiments.
A. (fig. 1.) is a solid block of very hard stone, 4 feet 4 inches
square, placed upon a bed of solid masonry, which descended
6 feet below the surface of the earth.   Upon this block of
stone, which served as a base to the whole machinery, was
placed the barrel B of hammered iron, upon its support C,
which is of cast brass, or rather of gun-metal; which support
was again placed upon a circular plate of hammered iron D,
8 inches in diameter, and $\frac{3}{4}$ of an inch thick, which last rested
upon the block of stone.   The opening of the bore of the barrel (which was placed in a vertical position, and which was
just $\frac{1}{4}$ of an inch in diameter) was closed by a solid hemisphere
E of hardened steel, whose diameter was 1.16 inch; and
upon this hemisphere the weight F, made use of for confining
the elastic fluid generated from the powder in its combustion,
reposed.   This weight, (which in some of the most interesting
experiments was a cannon of metal, a heavy twenty-four pounder,
placed vertically upon its cascabel) being fixed to the timbers
G G which formed a kind of carriage for it, was moveable up
and down; the ends of these timbers being moveable in grooves
cut in the vertical timbers K K, which being fixed below in
holes made to receive them in the block of stone, and above
by a cross piece L, were supported by braces and iron clamps
made fast to the thick walls of building of the arsenal.   This
weight was occasionally raised and lowered in the course of
the experiments (in placing and removing the barrel), by
means of a very strong lever, which is omitted in the drawing
to make it less complicated.   The barrel, a section of which is
represented in fig. 2. of its natural size, is 2.78 inches long,
and 2.82 inches in diameter, at its lower extremity, where it

reposes upon its supporter, but something less above, being somewhat diminished, and rounded off at its upper extremity. Its bore, which, as I have already observed, is $\frac{1}{4}$ of an inch in diameter, is 2.13 inches long, and it ends in a very narrow opening below, not more than 0.07 of an inch in diameter, and 1.715 inch long, which forms the vent (if I may be permitted to apply that name to a passage which is not open at both ends), by which the fire is communicated to the charge. From the centre of the bottom of the barrel there is a projection of about 0.45 of an inch in diameter, and 1.3 inch long, which forms the vent tube V. Fig. 3. is a view of an iron ball W, which being heated red-hot, and being applied to the vent tube by means of an hole O made in it for that purpose, fire is communicated through the solid substance of the vent tube to the powder it contains, and from thence to the charge.

Fig. 4. which is drawn on a scale of two inches to the inch, or half the real size of the machinery, shews how the barrel B was placed upon its support C; how this last was placed upon its circular plate of iron D, and how the red-hot iron ball W was applied to the vent tube V. This ball is managed by means of a long handle *b* of iron, and being introduced through a circular opening *g* in the support, and applied to the vent tube V, is kept in its place by means of a wedge, or rather lever *l*, whose external end is represented in the drawing as being broken off, to save room. The circular opening in front of the support is seen in front, and consequently more distinctly, in the drawing, fig. 1. In this drawing the end of the vent tube may be likewise discovered through this opening; but as it was necessary, in order to introduce all the parts of this machinery, to make the drawing upon a very small scale, it was not possible

to express all the smaller parts with that distinctness which I
wished. The other figures which are added, in which the parts
are expressed separately, and upon a larger scale, will, it is
hoped, supply this defect.

The stand, or support as I have called it, upon which the
barrel was placed, is circular, and in order that it might be united
more firmly to the plate of iron upon which it reposes, this
plate is furnished with a cylindrical projection *p*, 1 inch long
and 1½ in diameter, which enters a hole made in the bottom of
the stand to receive it.

Fig. 5. is a view of the barrel from above, in which the projecting screws, or rather cylinders, are seen, by which the hemisphere E, fig. 2. which closed the end of the barrel, was kept
in its place. Two of these screws 1, 2, are seen in the figures 2
and 4. The smaller circle *a b*, fig. 5. shews the diameter of a
circular plate of gold, which was let into the end of the barrel,
being firmly fixed to the iron solder; and the larger circle *c d*
represents a circular piece of oiled leather, which was placed
between the end of the barrel and the hemisphere which rested
upon it.

The end of the barrel was covered with gold, in order to
prevent as much as possible its being corroded by the elastic
vapour which, when the weight is not heavy enough to confine
it, escapes between the end of the barrel and the flat surface of
the hemisphere; but even this precaution was not found to be
sufficient to defend the apparatus from injury. The sharp edge
of the barrel at the mouth of the bore was worn away almost
immediately, and even the flat surface of the hemisphere, notwithstanding it was of hardened steel and very highly polished,
was sensibly corroded. This corrosion of the mouth of the

bore, by which the dimensions of the surface upon which the generated elastic fluid acted were rendered very uncertain, would alone have been sufficient to have rendered all my attempts to determine the force of fired gunpowder abortive, had I not found means to remedy the evil. The method I pursued for this purpose was as follows. Having provided some pieces of very good compact sole-leather, I caused them to be beaten upon an anvil with a heavy hammer, to render them still more compact; and then, by means of a machine made for that purpose, cylindric stoppers, of the same diameter precisely as the bore of the barrel, and 0.13 of an inch in length (that is to say, the thickness of the leather), were formed of it; and one of these stoppers, which had previously been greased with tallow, being put into the mouth of the piece after the powder had been introduced, and being forced into the bore till its upper end coincided with the end of the barrel, upon the explosion taking place, this stopper (being pressed on the one side by the generated elastic fluid, and on the other by the hemisphere, loaded with the whole weight employed to confine the powder), so completely closed the bore, that when the force of the powder was not sufficient to raise the weight to such a height that the stopper was actually blown out of the piece, not a particle of the elastic fluid could make its escape. And in those cases in which the weight was actually raised, and the generated elastic fluid made its escape, as it did not corrode the barrel in any other part but just *at the very extremity of the bore*, the experiment by which the weight was ascertained, which was just able to counterbalance the pressure of the generated elastic fluid, was in nowise vitiated, either by the increased diameter of the bore at its extremity, or by any

K k

corrosion of the hemisphere itself; for as long as the bore retained its form and its dimensions, in that part to which the
efforts of the elastic fluid were confined, that is, in that part of
the bore immediately in contact with the lower part of the
stopper, the experiment could not be affected by any imper-
fection of the bore either above or below.

In the figures 2. and 4. this stopper is represented in its place,
and fig. 6. shews the plan, and fig. 7. the profile of one of these
stoppers of its full size.   Fig. 8. shews a small but very useful
instrument, employed in introducing these stoppers into the
bore, and more especially in occasionally extracting them: it re-
sembles a common cork-screw, only it is much smaller.   In the
figure (where it is shewn in its full size), it is represented
screwed into a stopper.   Fig. 9. shews the plan, and fig. 10. a
side view, of the hemisphere of hardened steel, by which the
end of the barrel was closed.   In the figures 2. and 4. the barrel
is represented as being about half filled with powder.

Presuming that what has been already said, together with
the assistance of the annexed drawings, will be sufficient to
give a perfect idea of all the different parts of this apparatus, I
shall now proceed to give an account of the experiments which
from time to time have been made with it.   And in order to
render these details as intelligible as possible, and to shew the
results of all these inquiries in a clear and satisfactory manner,
I shall first give a brief account of the manner in which the
experiments were made; of the various precautions used;
and the particular appearances which were observed in the prosecution of them.

The powder made use of in these experiments was of the
best quality, being that kind called *poudre de chasse* by the

French, and very fine grained : and it was all taken from the same parcel. Care was taken to dry it very thoroughly, and the air of the room in which it was weighed out for use was very dry. The weights employed for weighing the powder were German apothecary's grains, 104.8 of which make 100 grains Troy. I have reduced the weights employed to confine the elastic vapour generated in the combustion of the powder from Bavarian pounds, in which they were originally expressed, to pounds avoirdupois. The measures of length were all taken in English feet and inches. The experiments were all made in the open air, in the court-yard of the arsenal at Munich; and they were all made in fair weather, and between the hours of nine and twelve in the forenoon, and two and five in the afternoon; but the barrel was always charged, and the extremity of the bore closed by its leather stopper, in the room where the powder was weighed. In placing the barrel upon the block of stone, great care was taken to put it exactly under the centre of gravity of the weight employed to confine the generated elastic vapour. Upon applying the red-hot ball to the vent tube, and fixing it in its place by its lever which supported it, the explosion very soon followed.

When the force of the generated elastic vapour was sufficient to raise the weight, the explosion was attended by a very sharp and surprisingly loud report; but when the weight was not raised, as also when it was only a little moved, but not sufficiently to permit the leather stopper to be driven quite out of the bore, and the elastic fluid to make its escape, the report was scarcely audible at the distance of a few paces, and did not at all resemble the report which commonly attends the explosion of gunpowder. It was more like the noise which attends the breaking of a small glass tube than any thing else to which I can compare it. In many of the experiments in which the elastic vapour was confined, this feeble report attending the explosion of the powder was immediately followed by another noise, totally different from it, which appeared to be occasioned by the falling back of the weight upon the end of the barrel, after it had been a little raised, but not sufficiently to permit the leather stopper to be driven quite out of the bore. In some of these experiments, a very small part only of the generated elastic fluid made its escape: in these cases the report was of a peculiar kind, and though perfectly audible at some considerable distance, yet not at all resembling the report of a musket. It was rather a very strong, sudden hissing, than a clear, distinct, and sharp report.

Though it could be determined with the utmost certainty by the report of the explosion, whether any part of the generated elastic fluid had made its escape, yet for still greater precaution, a light collar of very clean cotton wool was placed round the edge of the steel hemisphere, where it reposed upon the end of the barrel, which could not fail to indicate by the black colour it acquired, the escape of the elastic fluid, whenever it was strong enough to raise the weight by which it was confined sufficiently to force its way out of the barrel.

Though the end of the barrel at the mouth of the bore was covered with a circular plate of gold, in order the better to defend the mouth of the bore against the effects of the corrosive vapour, yet this plate being damaged in the course of the experiments (a piece of it being blown away), the remainder of it was removed; and it was never after thought necessary to replace it by another. When this plate of gold was taken away, the length of the barrel was of course diminished as much as the thickness of this plate amounted to, which was about $\frac{1}{400}$ part of an inch; but in order that even this small diminution of the length of the barrel might have no effect on the results of the experiments, its bore was deepened $\frac{1}{400}$ of an inch when this plate was removed, so that the *capacity* of the bore remained the same as before.

After making use of a great variety of expedients, the best and most convenient method of closing the end of the bore, and defending the flat surface of the steel hemisphere from the corroding vapours, was found to be this; first, to cover the end of the bore with a circular plate of thin oiled leather, then to lay upon this a very thin circular plate of hammered brass, and upon this brass plate the flat surface of the hemisphere. When the elastic fluid made its escape, a part of the leather was constantly found to have been torn away, but never in more places than one; that is to say, always on one side only.

What was very remarkable in all those experiments in which the generated elastic vapour was completely confined, was the small degree of expansive force which this vapour appeared to possess after it had been suffered to remain a few minutes, or even only a few seconds, confined in the barrel; for, upon raising the weight by means of its lever, and suffering this vapour to escape, instead of escaping with a loud report, it rushed out with a hissing noise hardly so loud or so sharp as the report of a common air-gun; and its efforts against the leathern stopper, by which it assisted in raising the weight, were so very feeble as not to be sensible. Upon examining the barrel, however, this diminution of the force of the generated elastic fluid was easily explained; for what was undoubtedly in the moment of the explosion in the form of an elastic fluid, was now found transformed into a *solid body* as hard as a stone! It may easily be imagined how much this unexpected appearance excited my curiosity; but, intent on the prosecution of the main design of these experiments, the ascertaining the force of fired gunpowder, I was determined not to permit myself to be enticed away from it by any extraordinary or unexpected appearances, or accidental discoveries, however alluring they might be; and faithful to this resolution, I postponed the examination of this curious phænomenon to a future period; and since that time I have not found leisure to engage in it. I think it right, however, to mention in this place such cursory observations as I was able, in the midst of my other pursuits, to make upon this subject; and it will afford me sincere pleasure, if what I have to offer should so far excite the curiosity of philosophers, as to induce some one who has leisure, and the means of pursuing such inquiries with effect, to precede me in the investigation of this interesting phænomenon; and as the subject is certainly not only extremely curious in itself, but bids fair to lead to other and very important discoveries, I cannot help flattering myself that some attention will be paid to it.   I have said that the solid substance into which the elastic vapour generated in the combustion of gunpowder was transformed, was *as hard as a stone.*   This I am sensible is but a vague expression; but the fact is, that it was very hard, and so firmly attached to the inside of the barrel, and particularly to the inside of the upper part of the vent tube, that it was always necessary, in order to remove it, to make use of a drill, and frequently to apply a considerable degree of force. This substance, which was of a black colour, or rather of a dirty grey, which changed to black upon being exposed to the air, had a pungent, acrid, alkaline taste, and smelt like liver of sulphur. It attracted moisture from the air with great avidity. Being moistened with water, and spirit of nitre being poured upon it, a strong effervescence ensued, attended by a very offensive and penetrating smell. Nearly the whole quantity of matter of which the powder was composed, seemed to have been transformed into this substance; for the quantity of elastic fluid which escaped upon removing the weight, was very inconsiderable; but this substance was *no longer gunpowder;* it was not even inflammable. What change had it undergone? what could it have lost? It is very certain the barrel was considerably heated in these experiments. Was this occasioned by the *caloric*, disengaged from the powder in its combustion, making its escape through the iron? And is this a proof of the existence of *caloric*, considered as a fluid *sui generis*; and that it actually enters into the composition of inflammable bodies, or of pure air, and is necessary to their combustion? I dare not take upon me to decide upon such important questions. I once thought that the heat acquired by a piece of ordnance in being fired, arose from the vibration or friction of its parts, occasioned by the violent blow it received in the explosion of the powder; but I acknowledge fairly, that it does not seem to be possible to account in a satisfactory manner for the very considerable degree of heat which the barrel acquired in these experiments, merely on that supposition.

That this hard substance, found in the barrel after an experiment in which the generated elastic vapour had been completely confined, was actually in a fluid or elastic state in the moment of the explosion, is evident from hence, that in all *those cases* in which the weight was raised, and the stopper blown out of the bore, nothing was found remaining in the barrel.   It was very remarkable that this hard substance was not found distributed about in all parts of the barrel indifferently, but there was always found to be more of it near the middle of the length of the bore, than at either of its extremities; and the upper part of the vent tube in particular was always found quite filled with it.   It should seem from hence, that it attached itself to those parts of the barrel which were soonest cooled; and hence the reason, most probably, why none of it was ever found in the lower part of the vent tube, where it was kept hot by the red-hot ball by which the powder was set on fire.

I found by a particular experiment, that the gunpowder made use of, when it was well shaken together, occupied rather less space in any given measure, than the same weight of water; consequently when gunpowder is fired in a confined space which it fills, the density of the generated elastic fluid must be at least equal to the density of water.   The real specific gravity of the solid grains of gunpowder, determined by weighing them in air and water, is to the specific gravity of water, as 1.868 to 1.000.   But if a measure, whose capacity is one cubic foot, hold 1000 ounces of water, the same measure will hold just 1077 ounces of fine grained gunpowder, such as I made use of in my experiments; that is to say, when it is well shaken together.   When it was moderately shaken together, I found its weight to be exactly equal to that of an equal volume, or rather measure, of water.   But it is evident that the weight of any given measure of gunpowder, must depend much upon the forms and sizes of its grains.   I shall add only one observation more, relative to the particular appearances which attended the experiments in which the elastic vapour generated in the combustion of gunpowder was confined, and that is, with regard to a curious effect produced upon the inferior flat surface of the leathern stopper, where it was in contact with the generated elastic vapour. Upon removing the stopper, its lower flat surface appeared entirely covered with an extremely white powder, resembling very light white ashes, but which almost instantaneously changed to the most perfect black colour upon being exposed to the air.

The sudden change of colour in this substance upon its being exposed to the air, has led me to suspect that the solid matter found in the barrel was not originally black, but that it became black merely in consequence of its being exposed to the air. The dirty grey colour it appeared to have immediately on being drilled out of the cavity of the bore, where it had fixed itself, seems to confirm this suspicion. An experiment made with a very strong glass barrel would not only decide this question, but would most probably render the experiment peculiarly beautiful and interesting on other accounts; and I have no doubt but a barrel of glass might be made sufficiently strong to withstand the force of the explosion. Whether it would be able to withstand the sudden effects of the heat, I own I am more doubtful; but as the subject is so very interesting, I think it would be worth while to try the experiment. Perhaps the apparatus might be so contrived as to set fire to the powder by the solar rays, by means of a common burning glass; but even if that method should fail, there are others equally unexceptionable, which might certainly be employed with success; and it is hardly possible to imagine any thing

L l

more curious than an experiment of this kind would be, if it were successful.

But to proceed to the experiments by which I endeavoured to ascertain the force of fired gunpowder. All the parts of the apparatus being ready, it was in the autumn of the year 1792 that the first experiment was made.

The barrel being charged with 10 grains of powder (its contents when quite full amounting to about 28 grains), and the end of the barrel being covered by a circular piece of oiled leather, and the flat side of the hemisphere being laid down upon this leather, and a heavy cannon, a twenty-four pounder, weighing 8081 lbs. avoirdupois, being placed upon its cascabel in a vertical position upon this hemisphere, in order to confine by its weight the generated elastic fluid, the heated iron ball was applied to the end of the vent tube; and I had waited but a very few moments in anxious expectation of the event, when I had the satisfaction of observing that the experiment had succeeded. The report of the explosion was extremely feeble, and so little resembling the usual report of the explosion of gunpowder, that the by-standers could not be persuaded that it was any thing more than a cracking of the barrel, occasioned merely by its being heated by the red-hot ball: yet, as I had been taught by the result of former experiments not to expect any other report, and as I found upon putting my hand upon the barrel that it began to be sensibly warm, I was soon convinced that the powder must have taken fire; and after waiting four or five minutes, upon causing the weight which rested upon the hemisphere to be raised, the confined elastic vapour rushed out of the barrel. Upon removing the barrel and examining it, its bore was found to be choaked up by the solid substance which I have already described, and from which it was with some difficulty that it was freed, and rendered fit for another experiment. The extreme feebleness of the report of the explosion, and the small degree of force with which the generated elastic fluid rushed out of the barrel upon removing the weight which had confined it, had inspired my assistants with no very favourable idea of the importance of these experiments. I had seen, indeed, from the beginning by their looks, that they thought the precautions I took to confine so inconsiderable a quantity of gunpowder as the barrel could contain, perfectly ridiculous; but the result of the following experiment taught them more respect for an agent, of whose real force they had conceived so very inadequate an idea.

In this second experiment, instead of 10 grains of powder, the former charge, the barrel was now quite filled with powder, and the steel hemisphere, with its oiled leather under it, was pressed down upon the end of the barrel by the same weight as was employed for that purpose in the first experiment, namely, a cannon weighing 8081 lbs. In order to give a more perfect idea of the result of this important experiment, it may not be amiss to describe more particularly one of the principal parts of the apparatus employed in it, I mean the barrel. This barrel (which though similar to it in all respects was not the same that has already been described,) was made of the best hammered iron, and was of uncommon strength. Its length was $2\frac{3}{4}$ inches; and though its diameter was also $2\frac{3}{4}$ inches, the diameter of its bore was no more than $\frac{1}{4}$ of an inch, or less than the diameter of a common goose quill. The length of its bore was 2.15 inches. Its diameter being $2\frac{3}{4}$ inches, and the diameter of its bore only $\frac{1}{4}$ of an inch, the thickness of the

metal was $1\frac{1}{4}$ inch; or, it was 5 times as thick as the diameter of its bore. The charge of powder was extremely small,
amounting to but little more than $\frac{1}{10}$ of a cubic inch; not so
much as would be required to load a small pocket pistol, and
not *one-tenth part* of the quantity frequently made use of for
the charge of a common musket. I should be afraid to relate
the result of this experiment, had I not the most indisputable
evidence to produce in support of the facts. This inconsiderable quantity of gunpowder, when it was set on fire by the
application of the red-hot ball to the vent tube, exploded with
such inconceivable force as to burst the barrel asunder in which
it was confined, notwithstanding its enormous strength; and
with such a loud report as to alarm the whole neighbourhood.
It is impossible to describe the surprise of those who were spec-
tators of this phænomenon. They literally turned pale with
affright and astonishment, and it was some time before they
could recover themselves. The barrel was not only completely
burst asunder, but the two halves of it were thrown upon the
ground in different directions : one of them fell close by my
feet, as I was standing near the machinery to observe more
accurately the result of the experiment. Though I thought it
possible that the weight might be raised, and that the generated elastic vapour would make its escape, yet the bursting of
the barrel was totally unexpected by me. It was a new lesson
to teach me caution in these dangerous pursuits.

It affords me peculiar satisfaction in laying these accounts
before the Royal Society, to be able to produce the most respectable testimony of their authenticity.

My friend Sir CHARLES BLAGDEN, one of the worthy Secre-
taries of the Society, visited Munich in the summer of the year

1793, in his return from Italy; and though I was then absent (travelling for the recovery of my health), yet, by my directions, he was not only shewn every part of the apparatus made use of in these experiments, but several experiments were actually repeated in his presence; and he was kind enough to take with him to England one half of the barrel which was burst in the experiment just mentioned, which at my request he has deposited in the Museum of the Society, and which I flatter myself will be looked upon as the most unequivocal proof of my discoveries relative to the amazing force of the elastic vapour generated in the combustion of gunpowder.

When the amazing strength of this barrel is considered, and when we consider the smallness of the capacity of its bore, it appears almost incredible, that so small a quantity of powder as that which was employed in the experiment could burst it asunder.

But without insisting on the testimony of several persons of respectable character, who were eye witnesses of the fact, and from whom Sir CHARLES BLAGDEN received a verbal account, in detail, of all the circumstances attending the experiment, I fancy I may very safely rest my reputation upon the silent testimony which this broken instrument will bear in my favour; much doubting whether it be in the power of art to burst asunder such a mass of solid iron, by any other means than those I employed.

Before I proceed to give an account of my subsequent experiments upon this subject, I shall stop here for a moment to make an estimate, from the known strength of iron, and the area of the fracture of the barrel, of the real force employed by the elastic vapour to burst it. In a course of experiments upon the strength of various bodies which I began many years ago,, and an account of which I intend at some future period to lay before the Royal Society,* I found, by taking the mean of the results of several experiments, that a cylinder of good tough hammered iron, the area of whose transverse section was only $\frac{3}{1600}$ of an inch, was able to sustain a weight of 119 lbs. avoirdupois, without breaking. This gives 63,466 lbs. for the weight which a cylinder of the same iron whose transverse section is one inch, would be able to sustain without being broken. The area of the fracture of the barrel before mentioned was measured with the greatest care, and was found to measure very exactly $6\frac{1}{2}$ superficial inches. If now we suppose the iron of which this barrel was formed, to be as strong as that whose strength I determined (and I have no reason to suspect it to be of an inferior quality), in that case, the force actually employed in bursting the barrel must have been equal to the pressure of a weight of 412529 lbs. For the resistance or cohesion of one inch, is to 63466 lbs. as that of $6\frac{1}{2}$ inches to 412529 lbs.; and this force, so astonishingly great, was exerted by a body which weighed less than 26 grains Troy, and which acted in a space that hardly amounted to $\frac{1}{10}$ of a cubic inch.

To compare this force exerted by the elastic vapour gene-

* Since writing the above, I have met with a misfortune which has put it out of my power to fulfil my promise to the Royal Society. On my return to England from Germany in October, 1795, after an absence of eleven years, I was stopped in my post-chaise in St. Paul's churchyard, in London, at six o'clock in the evening, and robbed of a trunk which was behind my carriage, containing all my private papers and my original notes and observations on philosophical subjects. By this cruel accident I have been deprived of the fruits of the labours of my whole life; and have lost all that I held most valuable. This most severe blow has left an impression on my mind, which I feel that nothing will ever be able entirely to remove.

rated in the combustion of gunpowder, and by which the barrel was burst, to the pressure of the atmosphere, it is necessary to determine the area of a longitudinal section of the bore of the piece. Now the diameter of the bore being $\frac{1}{4}$ of an inch, and its length (after deducting 0.15 of an inch for the length of the leathern stoppers) 2 inches, the area of its longitudinal section turns out to have been $\frac{1}{2}$ an inch. And if now we assume the mean pressure of the atmosphere $= 15$ lbs. avoirdupois for each superficial inch, this will give $7\frac{1}{2}$ for that upon a surface $= \frac{1}{2}$ inch, equal to the area of a longitudinal section of the bore of the barrel.

But we have just found that the force actually exerted by the elastic vapour in bursting the barrel, amounted to 412529 lbs.; this force was therefore 55004 times greater than the mean pressure of the atmosphere! For it is as $7\frac{1}{2}$ lbs. to 1 atmosphere, so 412529 lbs. to 55004 atmospheres.

Thinking it might perhaps be more satisfactory to know the real strength of the identical iron of which the barrel used in the before mentioned experiment was constructed, rather than to rest the determination of the strength of the barrel upon the decision of the strength of iron taken from another parcel, and which very possibly might be of a different quality, since writing the above, I have taken the trouble to ascertain the strength of the iron of which the barrel was made, which was done in the following manner. Having the one half of the barrel still in my possession, I caused small pieces, 2 inches long, and about $\frac{1}{8}$ of an inch square, to be cut out of the solid block, in the direction of its length, with a fine saw; and these pieces being first made round in their middle by filing, and then by turning in a lathe with a very sharp instrument, were reduced to such a size as was necessary, in order to their being pulled asunder in my machine for measuring the strength of bodies.   In this machine the body to be pulled asunder is held fast by two strong vices, the one fastened to the floor, and the other suspended to the short arm of a Roman balance, or common steel-yard; and in order that the bodies so suspended may not be injured by the jaws of the vices, so as to be weakened and to vitiate the experiments, they are not made cylindrical, but they are made larger at their two ends where they are held by the vices, and from thence their diameters were gradually diminished towards the middle of their lengths, where their measures were taken, and where they never failed to break.

As I had found by the results of many experiments which I had before made upon the strength of the various metals, that iron, as well as all other metals, is rendered much stronger by hammering, I caused those pieces of the barrel which were prepared for these experiments to be separated from the solid block of metal, and reduced to their proper sizes, by sawing, filing, and turning, and without ever receiving a single blow of a hammer; so that there is every reason to believe that the strength of the iron, as determined by the experiments, may safely be depended on.   The results of the experiments were as follows:

Experiments.	Diameter of the Cylinder at the Fracture.	Area of a transverse section of the Cylinder at the Fracture.	Weight required to break it. lbs. avoirdupois.	Weight required to break 1 inch of this iron. lbs. avoirdupois.
	Inch.	Inch.		
1.	$\frac{50}{1000}$	$\frac{1}{509,29}$	123.18	62737.
2.	$\frac{60}{1000}$	$\frac{1}{353,68}$	182.	64366.
3.	$\frac{66}{1000}$	$\frac{1}{292,3}$	220.75	64526.
4.	$\frac{76}{1000}$	$\frac{1}{220,7}$	277.01	61063.
Number of Experiments = 4.)				252692.
Mean				63173.

If now we take the strength of the iron of which the barrel was composed as here determined by actual experiments, and compute the force required to burst the barrel, it will be found equal to the pressure of a weight of $410624\frac{1}{2}$ lbs. instead of 436800 as before determined. For it is the resistance or force of cohesion of 1 inch of this iron to 63173 lbs., as that of $6\frac{1}{2}$ inches (the area of the fracture of the barrel) to $410624\frac{1}{2}$ lbs. And this weight turned into atmospheres, in the manner above described, gives 54750 atmospheres for the measure of the force which must have been exerted by the elastic fluid in bursting the barrel. But this force, enormous as it may appear, must still fall short of the real initial force of the elastic fluid generated in the combustion of gunpowder, before it has begun to expand; for it is more than probable that the barrel was in fact burst before the generated elastic fluid had exerted all its force, or that this fluid would have been able to have burst a barrel still stronger than that used in the experiment.—But I wave these speculations in order to hasten to more interesting and more satisfactory investigations. Passing over in silence a considerable number of promiscuous experiments, which having nothing particularly remarkable in their results, could throw no new light upon the subject, I shall proceed immediately to give an account of a regular set of experiments, undertaken with a view to the discovery of certain determined facts, and prosecuted with unremitting perseverance.

These experiments were made by my directions under the immediate care of Mr. REICHENBACH, commandant of the corps of artificers in the Elector's military service, and of Count SPRETI, first lieutenant in the regiment of artillery.

Though I was prevented by ill health from being actually present at all these experiments, yet being at hand, and having every day, and almost every hour, regular reports of the progress that was made in them, and of every thing extraordinary that happened, the experiments may be said with great truth to have been made under my immediate direction; and as the two gentlemen by whom I was assisted, were not only every way qualified for such an undertaking, but had been present, and had assisted me in a number of similar experiments which I had myself made, they had acquired all that readiness and dexterity in the various manipulations which are so useful and necessary in experimental inquiries; and I think I can safely venture to say that the experiments may be depended upon. It would have afforded me great satisfaction to have been able to say that the experiments were all made by myself; and I had resolved to repeat them before I made them public, particularly as there appear to have been some very extraordinary and quite unaccountable differences in the results of those made in different seasons of the year; but having hitherto been prevented by ill health, and by other avocations, from engaging again in these laborious researches, I have thought it right not to delay any longer the publication of facts, which appear to me to be both new and interesting, as their publication may perhaps excite others to engage in their farther investigation.

The principal objects I had in view in the following set of experiments were, first, to determine the expansive force of the elastic vapour generated in the combustion of gunpowder in its various states of condensation, and to ascertain the ratio of its elasticity to its density : and secondly, to measure, by one decisive experiment, the utmost force of this fluid in its most dense state; that is to say, when the powder completely fills the space in which it is fired, and in which the generated fluid is confined. As these experiments were very numerous, and as it will be more satisfactory to be able to see all their results at one cursory view, I have brought them into the form of a general table.

In this table, which does not stand in need of any particular explanation, may be seen the results of all these investigations.

The dimensions of the barrel made use of in the experiments mentioned in this table, were as follows.

Diameter of the bore at its muzzle $=$ 0.25 of an inch.

Joint capacities of the bore, and of its vent tube, exclusive of the space occupied by the leathern stopper, $=$ 0.08974 of a cubic inch.

Quantity of powder contained by the barrel and its vent tube when both were quite full, (exclusive of the space occupied by the leathern stopper,) 25.641 German apothecary's grains, $=$ $24\frac{1}{2}$ grains Troy.

The capacities of the barrel and of its vent tube were determined by filling them with mercury, and then weighing in air and in water the quantity of mercury required to fill them; and the quantity of powder required to fill the barrel and its vent tube was determined by computation, from the known joint capacities of the barrel and its vent tube, in parts of a cubic inch, and from the known specific gravity of the powder used in the experiments.

Thus the contents of the barrel and its vent tube having been found to amount to 0.08974 of a cubic inch, and it having been found that 1 cubic inch of the gunpowder in question, well shaken together, weighed just 272.68 grains Troy, this gives 24.47 grains Troy (= 25.641 grains, German apothecary's weight) for the contents of the barrel and its vent tube.

The numbers expressing the charges of powder in *thousandth parts* of the joint capacities of the barrel and of its vent tube, were determined from the known quantities of powder used in the different experiments, expressed in German apothecary's grains, and the relation of these quantities to the quantity required to fill the barrel and its vent tube completely.

Thus, as the barrel and its vent tube were capable of containing 25.641 apothecary's grains of powder, if we suppose this quantity to be divided into 1000 equal parts, this will give 39 of those parts for 1 grain; 78 parts for 2 grains; 390 for 10 grains, &c. For it is 25.641 to 1000, as 1 to 39 very nearly.

As this method of expressing the quantities of powder shows at the same time the relative density of the generated elastic fluid, it is the more satisfactory on that account: it will also considerably facilitate the computations necessary in order to ascertain the ratio of the elasticity of this fluid to its density.

The elastic force of the fluid generated in the combustion of the charge of powder, is measured by the weight by which it was confined, or rather by that which it was just able to move, but which it could not raise sufficiently to blow the leathern stopper quite out of the mouth of the bore of the barrel.

This weight in all the experiments, except those which were made with very small charges of powder, was a piece of ordnance, of greater or less dimensions, or greater or less weight, according to the force of the charge; placed vertically upon its cascabel, upon the steel hemisphere which closed the end of the barrel; and the same piece of ordnance, by having its bore filled with a greater or smaller number of bullets, as the occasion required, was made to serve for several experiments.

The weight employed for confining the generated elastic fluid, is expressed in the following table in *pounds avoirdupois*; but in order that a clearer and more perfect idea may be formed of the real force of its elastic fluid, I have added a column in which its force, answering to each charge of powder, is expressed in *atmospheres*.

The numbers in this column were computed in the following manner. The diameter of the bore of the barrel at its muzzle being just $\frac{1}{4}$ of an inch, the area of its transverse section is 0.049088 of a superficial inch; and assuming the mean pressure of the atmosphere upon 1 superficial inch equal to 15 lbs. avoirdupois, this will give 0.73631 of a pound avoirdupois for that pressure upon 0.049088 of a superficial inch, or upon a surface equal to the area by which the generated elastic fluid acted on the weight employed to confine it; consequently the weight expressed in *pounds avoirdupois*, which measured thè force of the generated elastic fluid in any given experiment, being divided by 0.73631, will show how many times the pressure exerted by the fluid was greater than the mean pressure of the atmosphere. Thus in the experiment, No. 6, where the weight which measured the elastic force of the generated fluid was = 504.8 lbs. avoirdupois, it is $\frac{504.8}{0.73631} = 685.6$ atmospheres. And so of the rest.

I have said that the diameter of the bore of the barrel, made use of in the following experiments, was just $\frac{1}{4}$ of an inch *at its muzzle*, and this is strictly true, as I found upon measuring it with the greatest care; but its diameter is not perfectly the same throughout its whole length, being rather narrower towards its lower end: yet the *capacity* of the barrel being known, and also *the diameter of the bore of its muzzle*, any small inequalities of the bore in any other part can in no wise affect the results of the experiments, as will be evident to those who will take the trouble to consider the matter for a moment with attention. I should not indeed have thought it necessary to mention this circumstance, had I not been afraid that some one who should calculate the joint capacities of the bore and of the vent tube from their lengths and diameters, finding their calculation not to agree with my determination of those capacities, as ascertained by filling them with mercury, might suspect me of having committed an error. The mean diameter of the bore of the barrel, as determined from its length and its capacity, turns out to be just 0.2281 of an inch; the diameter of the vent tube being taken equal to 0.07 of an inch, and its length 1.715 inch.

Table I. Experiments on the Force of fired Gunpowder.

No. of the Experiment	Time when the Experiment was made. 1793.	State of the Atmosphere		The charge of Powder		Weight employed to confine the elastic Fluid.		General Remarks.
		Thermom.	Barometer.	In Apoth. gr.	In 1000 parts of the capacity of the bore.	In lbs. avoirdupois.	In atmospheres.	
N°	h. m.	F.	Engl. In.	grs	Parts.	lbs.		
1	23d Feb. 9 0	31°	28.58	1	39	504.8	—	⎰ The generated elastic fluid
2	9 30	—	—	2	78	—		⎱ was completely confined, the weight not being raised
3	25th 9 0	37°	28.56	3	117	—		Ditto.
4	10 15	—	—	4	156	—		Ditto, weight not raised.
5	10 30	—	—	5	195	—		Ditto, ditto.
6	11 0	—	—	6	234	—	685.6	Weight just moved.
7	3 0 PM	57°	28.37	1	39	14.16		⎰ In these three experiments
8	3 15					26.5		⎱ the weight was raised with a report as loud as that of
9	3 30					38.9		a pistol.
10	3 45					51.3		⎰ But just raised, report much weaker.
11	4 0	—	—			57.4	77.86	Weight hardly moved.
12	26th 9 0	34°	28.1	2	78	163.5		Not raised.
13	9 15					124		Raised with a loud report.
14	9 30					130.5		Ditto, the report weaker.
15	9 45					133		Ditto, the report still weaker.
16	10 0	—	—			134.2	182.3	Weight but just moved.
17	3 0	48°	28.31	3	117	186.3		Raised with a loud report.
18	3 15					198.7		Ditto, ditto.
19	3 30					204.8		Ditto, report weaker.
20	3 45					208.5		Raised, report weaker.
21	4 0	—	—			212.24	288.2	⎰ The weight hardly moved, no report.
22	27th 3 0	50°	28.36	4	156	269.2		Raised with a loud report.
23	3 15					274.13		Ditto, ditto.
24	3 30					277.9		Ditto, report less loud.
25	3 45					281.57	382.4	⎰ Weight hardly moved, and no report.
26	28th 9 0	34°	28.32	5	195	319.68		Raised, loud report.
27	9 15					351.37		Ditto, ditto.
28	9 30					400.9		Ditto, ditto.
29	10 0					475.2		Not raised.
30	3 0	48°	28.35			443.5		Not raised.
31	3 15	—	—			425.65		Not raised.
32	3 30					419.46		Not raised.

Table I.   Experiments on the Force of fired Gunpowder.

No. of the Experiment.	Time when the Experiment was made. 1793.	State of the Atmosphere.		The charge of Powder.		Weight employed to confine the elastic Fluid.		General Remarks.
		Thermom.	Barometer.	In Apoth. gr.	In 1000 parts of the capacity of the bore.	In lbs. avoirdupois.	In atmospheres.	
	h. m.	F.	Eng. In.	grs	Parts.	lbs.		
33	28th Feb. 3 45	48°	28.35	5	195	413.27	561.2	Weight but just moved.
34	1st Mar. 9 0	34°	28.35	7	273	535.79		Raised with a loud report.
35	9 15	—	—	—	—	548.14		Ditto, ditto.
36	9 30	—	—	—	—	560.52		Ditto, ditto.
37	3 0	59°	28.34	—	—	572.9		Ditto, ditto.
38	3 15	—	—	—	—	585.28		Ditto, report weaker.
39	3 30	—	—	—	—	597.66	811.7	{ Weight but just moved, no report.
40	3 45	—	—	8	312	690.52		Raised, report very loud.
41	4 0	—	—	—	—	752.42		Ditto, ditto.
42	4 15	—	—	—	—	783.37		Ditto, ditto.
43	2d 9 0	50°	28.32	—	—	876.22		Not raised.
44	9 15	—	—	—	—	845.19		But just raised, report weak.
45	9 30	—	—	—	—	857.64	1164.8	{ Weight but just moved, and no report.
46	9 45	—	—	9	351	961.65		Raised with a loud report.
47	10 0	—	—	—	—	1209.4		Not raised.
48	10 30	—	—	—	—	1142.3	1551.3	{ Weight just moved, no report.
49	3 0	52°	28.33	10	390	1456.8		Not raised.
50	3 30	—	—	—	—	1329.9		Raised, loud report.
51	5th 9 0	32°	28.2	—	—	1387.5	1884.3	{ Weight but just moved, and no report.
52	9 15	—	—	11	429	1708.2		Not raised.
53	9 45	—	—	—	—	1646.2		Not raised.
54	10 15	—	—	—	—	1615.2		Raised, with a weak report.
55	10 45	—	—	—	—	1634	2219	{ Weight but just moved, and no report.
56	6th 9 0	36°	28.34	12	468	1943.3		Not raised.
57	9 30	—	—	—	—	1932.2		Not raised.
58	10 30	—	—	—	—	1907.4		Weight not raised.
59	11 0	—	—	—	—	1878.4		Raised with a loud report.
60	11 30	—	—	—	—	1895.1	2573.7	{ Weight but just moved, and no report.
61	3 0	42°	28.3	13	507	2142.7		Raised with a loud report.
62	3 15	—	—	—	—	2204.6		Ditto, ditto.

Table I. Experiments on the Force of fired Gunpowder.

No. of the Experiment.	Time when the Experiment was made. 1793.	State of the atmosphere.		The charge of Powder.		Weight employed to confine the elastic Fluid.		General Remarks.
		Thermom.	Barometer.	Apoth, grs.	In 1000 parts of the capacity of the bore.	In lbs. avoirdupois.	In atmospheres.	
N°	h. m.	F.	Eng. In.	grs	Parts.	lbs.		
63	6th Mar. 3 30	42°	28.3	13	507	2266.5		Raised with a loud report.
64	3 45	—	·	—	—	2390.3		Raised, report weaker.
65	4 0	—	—	—	—	2422	3288.3	Weight just moved, no report.
66	9th 9 0	43°	28.31	14	546	3213		Not raised.
67	9 30	—	—	—	—	3093		Not raised.
68	10 0	—	—	—	—	2968		Not raised.
69	10 30	—	—	—	—	2846		Raised, with a loud report.
70	10 45	—	—	—	—	2908		Raised, report weaker.
71	11 0	—	—	—	—	2939		Ditto, report still weaker.
72	11 15	—	—	—	—	2951	4008	Weight but just moved, no report.
73	11 30	—	—	15	585	3750		Not raised.
74	11 45	—	—	—	—	3508		Not raised.
75	12 15	—	—	—	·	3477	4722.5	Weight but just moved, and no report.
76	11th 9 0	43°	28.3	16	624	4037		The weight was raised with a loud report.
77	9 15	—	—	—	·	4284		Raised, loud report.
78	9 30	—	—	—	—	4532		Ditto, ditto.
79	4th Apr. 3 0	70°	28.2	—	—	5027		Ditto, ditto.
80	3 15	—	—	—	—	5138		Raised, report weaker.
81	3 30	—	—	—	—	5262		Not raised.
82	3 45	—	—	—	—	5220	7090	Weight just moved, but no report.
83	5th 3 0	68°	28.3	17	663	8081		Not raised.
84	3 30	—	—	18	702	8081	10977	The weight was raised with a very sharp report, louder than that of a well loaded musket.
85	4 0	—	—	—	—	8700		The vent tube of the barrel was burst, the explosion being attended with a very loud report.

The barrel being rendered unfit for further service, by the bursting of its vent tube, an end was put to this set of experiments.

In order that a clear and satisfactory idea may be formed of the results of these experiments I have drawn the figure (Tab. VI.), in which the given densities of the generated elastic fluid, or (which amounts to the same thing) the quantities of powder used for the charge, being taken on the line A B, from A towards B, the corresponding elasticities, as found by the experiments, are represented by lines perpendicular to the line AB, at the points where the measures of the densities end.

As the irregularities of the dotted line A C are owing, no doubt, merely to the errors committed in making the experiments, these irregularities being removed, by drawing the line A D in such a manner as to balance the errors of the experiments, this line A D, which must necessarily be regular, will, by bare inspection, give us a considerable degree of insight into the nature of the equation which must be formed to express the relation of the densities to the elasticities; one principal object of these experimental inquiries.

Putting the density $= x$, and the elasticity $= y$, the line A D will be the locus of the equation expressing the relation of x to y; and had Mr. Robins's supposition, that the elasticity is as the density, been true, x would have been found to be to y in a constant (simple) ratio, A D would have been a straight line, and A E would have been the position of this line, had Mr. Robins's determination of the force of fired gunpowder been accurate.

But A D is a curve, and this shows that the ratio of x to y

is variable; and moreover it is a curve *convex towards the line* A B, on which x is taken; and this circumstance proves that the ratio of y to x is continually increasing.

Though these experiments all tend to show that the ratio of y to x increases as x is increased, yet when we consider the subject with attention, we shall, I think, find reason to conclude that the exponent of that ratio can never be less than *unity;* and farther, that it must of necessity have *that value precisely,* when, the density being taken infinitely small, or $= 0$, x and y vanish together.

Supposing this to be the case, namely, that the exponent of the ultimate ratio of y to x is $= 1$, let the densities or successive values of x be expressed by a series of natural numbers,

$$0, \ 1, \ 2, \ 3, \ 4, \ \&c. \text{ to } 1000,$$

the last term $= 1000$ answering to the greatest density; or when the powder completely fills the space in which it is confined; then, by putting $z =$ the variable part of the exponent of the ratio of y to x,

To each of the successive } values of $x =$ } $0, \ 1, \ 2, \ 3, \ 4, \ \&c.$

The corresponding value } of y will be accurately ex- } $0^{1+z}, \ 1^{1+z}, \ 2^{1+z}, \ 3^{1+z}, \ 4^{1+z}, \ \&c.$ pressed by the equations }

For, as the variable part (z), of this exponent may be taken of *any dimensions,* it may be so taken at each given term of the series, (or for each particular value of x), that the equation $x^{1+z} = y$, may always correspond with the result of the experiments; and when this is done, the value of z, and the law of its increase as x increases, will be known; and this will show the relation of x to y, or of the elasticities of the generated fluid to their corresponding densities, in a clear and satisfactory manner.

Without increasing the length of this paper still more (it being perhaps already too voluminous), by giving an account in detail of all the various computations I made, in order, from the results of the experiments in the foregoing table, to ascertain the real value of z, and the rate at which it increases as x is increased, I shall content myself with merely giving the general results of these investigations, and referring for farther information to the following table II, where the agreement of the law founded on them, with the results of the foregoing experiments, may be seen.

Having from the results of the experiments in table I. computed the different values of z, corresponding to all the different densities, or different charges of powder, from 1 grain, or 39 *thousandth parts*, to 18 grains, or 702 *thousandth parts* of the capacity of the barrel, I found that while the density of the elastic fluid $= x$, expressed in *thousandth parts*, is increased from 0 to 1000 (or till the powder completely fills the space in which it is confined), the variable part z of the exponent of x, $(1 + z)$ is increased from 0 to $\frac{4}{10}$. And though some of the experiments, and particularly those which were made with large charges of powder, seemed to indicate that while x is increased with an equable or uniform motion, z increases with a motion continually accelerated; *yet*, as the results of by far the greatest number of the other experiments showed the velocity of the increase of z to be *equable*, this circumstance, added to some other reasons drawn from the nature of the subject, have induced me to assume the ratio of the increase of z to the increase of x as constant.

But if, while x increases with an equable velocity from o to 1000, z is increased with an *equable velocity* from o to $\frac{4}{10}$, then it is every where z to x as $\frac{4}{10}$ to 1000; or $1000\,z = \frac{4}{10}$, and consequently $z = \frac{4x}{10000}$; and when x is $= 1$, it is $z = \frac{4}{10000}$ $= 0.0004$; and when x is greater or less than 1, it is $z = 0.0004x$; and z being expunged, the general equation expressing the relation of x to y becomes $x^{1+0.0004x} = y$; and this is the equation which was made use of in computing the values of y, as expressed in the following table.

In order that the elasticities might be expressed in atmospheres, the values of y, as determined by this equation, were multiplied by 1.841.

If it be required to express the elasticity in *pounds avoirdupois*, then the value of y, as determined by the foregoing equation, being multiplied by 27.615, will show how many pounds avoirdupois, pressing upon a superficial inch, will be equal to the pressure exerted by the elastic fluid in the case in question.

Table II.   General Results of the Experiments in Table I. on the Force of fired Gunpowder.

The Charge of Powder.		Value of the Exponent $1+0.0004\,x$.	Computed Elasticity of the generated Fluid, or Value of y, according to the Theorem $x^{1+0.0004\,x} = y$.		Actual Elasticity, as shown by the Experiments.	Difference of the computed and the actual Elasticities.
In Grains.	In equal Parts.		In equal Parts.	In Atmospheres.	In Atmospheres.	In Atmospheres.
1	39	1.0156	41.294	76.822	77.86	+ 1.838
2	78	1.0312	89.357	164.506	182.30	+ 17.794
3	117	1.0468	146.210	269.173	228.2	− 40.973
4	156	1.0624	213.784	393.577	382.4	− 11.177
5	195	1.0780	294.209	541.640	561.2	+ 19.560
6	234	1.0936	389.919	717.841	685.6	− 32.241
7	273	1.1092	503.723	927.353	811.7	− 115.653
8	312	1.1248	638.889	1176.19	1164.8	− 12.390
9	351	1.1404	799.223	1471.37	1551.3	+ 79.930
10	390	1.1560	989.169	1821.06	1884.3	+ 63.240
11	429	1.1716	1213.91	2234.81	2219.	− 15.810
12	468	1.1872	1479.50	2723.77	2573.7	− 150.07
13	507	1.2028	1793.	3300.91	3283.3	− 17.61
14	546	1.2184	2162.69	3980.52	4008.	+ 27.48
15	585	1.2340	2598.18	4783.26	4722.5	− 60.76
16	624	1.2496	3110.73	5726.83	7090.	+1363.17
17	663	1.2652	3713.46	6836.46		
18	702	1.2808	4421.69	8140.34	10977.	+2836.66
19	741	1.2964	5253.3	9671.33		
20	780	1.3120	6229.14	11467.8		
25.641	1000	1.4000	15848.9	29177.9		

The agreement of the elasticities computed from the theorem $x^{1+0.0004\,x} = y$, with the actual elasticities as they were measured in the experiments, may be seen in the foregoing table; but this agreement may be seen in a much more striking manner by a bare inspection of the figure (Tab. VI.); for the line A D in this figure having been drawn from the computed elasticities, its general coincidence with the line A C shows how nearly the computed and the actual elasticities approach each other. And when the irregularities of the line A C (which, as had already been observed, must be attributed to the unavoidable errors of the experiments), are corrected, these two curves will be found to coincide with much precision throughout a considerable part of the range of the experiments; but towards the end of the set of experiments, when the charges of powder were considerably increased, the elasticities seem to have increased faster than, according to the assumed law, they ought to have done. From this circumstance, and from the immense force the charge must have exerted in the experiment, when the barrel was burst, I was led to suspect that the elastic force of the fluid generated in the combustion of gunpowder, when its density is great, is still much greater than these experiments seem to indicate; and a farther investigation of the subject served to confirm me in this opinion.

It has been shown that the force exerted by the charge in the experiment in which the barrel was burst could not have been less than the pressure of 54,752 atmospheres; but the greatest force of the generated elastic fluid, when, the powder filling the space in which it is confined, its density is $= 1000$, on computing its elasticity by the theorem $x^{1+0.0004\,x} = y$, turns out to be only equal to 29,178 atmospheres.

In this computation the mean of the results of all the experiments in the foregoing set is taken as a standard to ascertain the value, expressed in atmospheres, of y, and it is $y \times 1.841 = 29,178$.

But if, instead of taking the mean of the whole set of experiments as a standard, we select that experiment in which the force exerted by the powder appears to have been the greatest, yet in this case even the initial force of fired gunpowder, computed by the above rule, would be much too small.

In the experiment No. 84, when the charge consisted of 18 grains of powder, and the density or value of x was 702, a weight equal to the pressure of 10,977 atmospheres was raised. Here the value of y ($= x^{1+0.0004x}$) is found to be ($702^{1.2808}$), $= 4421.7$; and to express this value of y in atmospheres, and at the same time to accommodate it to the actual result of the experiment, it must be multiplied by 2.4826; for it is 4421.7 (the value of y expressed in equal parts) to 10,977 (its value in atmospheres, as shown by the experiment), as 1 to 2.4826, and consequently $4421.7 \times 2.4826 = 10,977$.

If now the value of y be computed on the same principles, when x is put $= 1000$, it will turn out to be $y = 1000^{1+0.4}$ $= 15,849$; and this number expressed in atmospheres, by multiplying it by 2.4826, gives the value of $y = 39,346$ atmospheres.

This however falls still far short of 54,752 atmospheres, the force the powder was actually found to exert when the charge filled the space in which it was confined. But in the 84th experiment, when 18 grains of powder were used, as the weight (8081 lbs. avoirdupois) was raised with *a very loud report*, it is more than probable that the force of the generated elastic fluid was in fact considerably greater than that at which it was estimated, namely, greater than the pressure of 10,977 atmospheres.

But, without wasting time in fruitless endeavours to reconcile anomalous experiments, which, probably, never can be made to agree, I shall hasten to give an account of another set of experiments; the results of which, it must be confessed, were still more various, extraordinary, and inexplicable.

The machinery having been repaired and put in order, the experiments were recommenced in July, 1793, the weather at that time being very hot.

The principal part of the apparatus, *the barrel*, had undergone a trifling alteration : upon refitting and cleaning it, the diameter of its bore at the muzzle was found to be a little increased, so that a weight equal to 8081 lbs. avoirdupois, instead of being equal to 10977 atmospheres (as was the case in the former experiments), was now just equal to the pressure of 9431 atmospheres.

Though I was not at Munich when this last set of experiments was made, they however were undertaken at my request, and under my direction, and I have no reason to doubt of their having been executed with all possible care. They were all made by the same persons who were employed in making the first set; and as these experimenters may be supposed to have grown expert in practice, and as they could not possibly have had any interest in deceiving me, I cannot suspect the accuracy of their reports.

Table III. Experiments on the Force of fired Gunpowder.

No. of the Experiment.	Time when the Experiment was made. 1793.	State of the Atmosphere.		The Charge of Powder.		Weight employed to confine the elastic Fluid.		General Remarks.
		Thermom.	Barometer.	In Apoth. grs.	In 1000 parts of the capacity of the bore.	In lbs. avoirdupois	In atmospheres.	
		F.	Eng. In.	grs.	Parts.	lbs.		
N° 86	1st July 4 0	88°	28.37	17	663	8081	9431	{ The weight was raised with an astonishing loud report.
87	4 30	—	—	—	—	—		{ In these three experiments
88	4 45	—	—	16	624	—		the weight was raised with
89	5 0	—	—	15	585	—		a very loud report.
90	5 30	—	—	12	468	—		Weight not raised.
91	6 0	—	—	13	507	—	9431	{ Weight but just raised, report very weak.
92	2d 9 0	71°	28.38	—	—	—		Raised, loud report.
93	9 30	—	—	12	468	—		Raised, feeble report.
94	10 0	—	—	—	—	—	9431	Raised, report very feeble.
95	10 30	80°	—	11⅞	—	—		*Just moved,* no report.
96	3d 10 0	70°	28.55	12	468	—		Not raised.
97	10 30	—	—	13	507	—		Not raised.
98	11 0	75°	—	14	546	—	9431	Just raised, feeble report.
99	4th 9 0	70°	28.56	14	546	—		Not raised.
100	9 30	—	—	—	—	—		Not raised.
101	10 0	72°	—	15	585	—		{ The weight was raised, the report not very loud.
102	10 30	—	—	15½	—	—		Nearly as above.
103	8th 9 0	74°	28.42	—	—	—		{ Raised, and with an uncommonly loud report.
104	9 30	—	—	13	507	—		Raised, report very loud.
105	10 45	85°	—	12	468	—	9431	{ But just raised, the report very feeble.
106	17th 9 0	75°	28.4	—	—	—		Nearly as above.
107	9 45	—	—	—	—	—		Not raised.
108	10 30	—	—	11¼	—	—		*Just moved,* no report.
109	11 0	—	—	—	—	—		The same as above.

It appears from the foregoing table, that in the afternoon of the 1st of July, the weight (which was a heavy brass cannon, a 24 pounder, weighing 8081 lbs. avoirdupois), was not raised by 12 grains of powder, but that 13 grains raised it with an audible though weak report. That the next morning, July 2d, at 10 o'clock, it was raised twice by charges of 12 grains. That in the morning of the 3d of July, it was not raised by 12 grains, nor by 13 grains; but that 14 grains just raised it. That in the afternoon of the same day, two experiments were made with 14 grains of powder, in neither of which the weight was raised; but that in another experiment, in which 15 grains of powder were used, it was raised with a moderate report. That in the morning of the 8th July, in two experiments, one with 15 grains, and the other with 13 grains of powder, the weight was raised with a *loud report*; and in an experiment with 12 grains, it was raised with a *feeble report*. And lastly, that in three successive experiments, made in the morning of the 17th of July, the weight was raised by charges of 12 grains.

Hence it appears, that under circumstances the most favourable to the developement of the force of gunpowder, a charge (= 12 grains) filling $\frac{468}{1000}$ of the cavity in which it is confined, on being fired, exerts a force against the sides of the containing vessel equal to the pressure of 9431 atmospheres; which pressure amounts to 141465 lbs. avoirdupois on each superficial inch.

Mr. ROBINS makes the initial, or greatest force of the fluid generated in the combustion of gunpowder, (namely when the charge completely fills the space in which it is confined), to be only equal to the pressure of 1000 atmospheres. It appears, however, from the result of these experiments, that even admitting the elasticities to be as the densities, as Mr. ROBINS supposes them to be, the initial force of this generated elastic fluid must be at least twenty times greater than Mr. ROBINS determined it; for $\frac{468}{1000}$, the density of the elastic fluid in the experiments in question, is to 1, its density when the powder quite fills the space in which it is confined, as 9431 atmospheres, the measure of its elastic force in the experiments in question, to 20108 atmospheres; which, according to Mr. ROBINS's theory respecting the ratio of the elasticities to the densities, would be the measure of its initial force.

But all my experiments tend uniformly to prove, that the elasticities increase *faster* than in the simple ratio of the corresponding densities; consequently the initial force of the generated elastic fluid *must necessarily* be greater than the pressure of 20108 atmospheres.

In one of my experiments which I have often had occasion to mention, the force actually exerted by the fluid must have been at least equal to the pressure of 54752 atmospheres. The other experiments ought, no doubt, to show, at least, that it is *possible* that such an enormous force may have been exerted by the charge made use of; and this, I think, they actually indicate.

In the first set of experiments, which were made when the weather was cold, though the results of them uniformly showed the force of the powder to be much less than it appeared to be in all the subsequent experiments, made with greater charges, and in warm weather, yet they all show that the ratio of the elasticity of the generated fluid to its density is very different from that which Mr. Robins's theory supposes; and that this ratio increases as the density of the fluid is increased.

Supposing (what on many accounts appears to be extremely probable) that this ratio increases uniformly, or with an equable celerity, while the density is uniformly augmented; and supposing farther, that the velocity and limit of its increase have been rightly determined from the result of the set of experiments, table I. which were made with that view; then, from the result of the experiments of which we have just been giving an account, (in which 12 grains of powder exerted a force equal to 9431 atmospheres), taking these experiments as a standard, we can with the help of the theorem $(x^{1+0.0004\,x}=y)$ deduced from the former set of experiments, compute the initial force of fired gunpowder, thus :

The density of the elastic fluid, when 12 grains of powder are used for the charge, being $=468$, it is $468^{1.1871}=y=1479.5$; and in order that this value of y may correspond with the result of the experiment, and be expressed in atmospheres, it must be multiplied by a certain coefficient, which will be found by dividing the value of y expressed in atmospheres, as shown by the experiment, by the number here found indicating its value, as determined by computation.

It is therefore $\frac{9431}{1479.5}=6.3744$ for the value of this coefficient, and this multiplied into the number 1479.5 gives 9431 for the value of y in atmospheres.

Again, the density being supposed $=1000$ (or, that the charge of powder completely fills the cavity in which it is confined), in that case it will be $1000^{1+0.4}=y=15849$; and this number being turned into atmospheres by being multiplied by the coefficient above found ($=6.3744$), gives 101021 atmospheres for the measure of the initial force of the elastic fluid generated in the combustion of gunpowder.

Enormous as this force appears, I do not think it over-rated; for nothing much short of such an inconceivable force can, in my opinion, ever explain in a satisfactory manner the bursting of the barrel so often mentioned; and to this we may add, that, as in 7 different experiments, all made with charges of 12 grains of powder, there were no less than 5 in which the weight was *raised with a report,* and as the same weight was *moved* in 3 different experiments in which the charge consisted of less than 12 grains, there does not appear to be any reason whatever for doubt with regard to the principal fact on which the above computation is founded.

There is an objection, however, that may be made to these decisions respecting the force of gunpowder, which, on the first view, appears of considerable importance; but on a more careful examination it will be found to have no weight.

If the force of fired gunpowder is so very great, how does it happen that fire-arms and artillery of all kinds, which certainly are not calculated to withstand so enormous a force, are not always burst when they are used? I might answer this question by another, by asking how it happened that the barrel used in my experiments, and which was more than ten times stronger in proportion to the size of its bore than ever a piece of ordnance was formed, could be burst by the force of gunpowder, if its force is not in fact much greater than it has ever been supposed to be? But it is not necessary to have recourse to such a shift to get out of this difficulty: there is nothing more to do than to show, which may easily be done, that the combustion of gunpowder is less rapid than it has hitherto been supposed to be, and the objection in question falls to the ground.

Mr. Robins's theory supposes that all the powder of which a charge consists is not only set on fire, but that it is actually *consumed* and " *converted into an elastic fluid before the bullet* " *is sensibly moved from its place.*" I have already in the former part of this paper offered several reasons which appeared to me to prove that, though the *inflammation* of gunpowder is very rapid, yet the progress of the combustion is by no means so *instantaneous* as has been imagined. I shall now give an account of some experiments which put that matter out of all doubt.

It is a fact well known that on the discharge of fire-arms of all kinds, cannon and mortars as well as muskets, there is always a considerable quantity of unconsumed grains of gunpowder blown out of them; and, what is very remarkable, and as it leads directly to a discovery of the cause of this effect is highly deserving of consideration, these unconsumed grains are not merely blown out of the *muzzles* of fire-arms; they come out also by their vents or touch-holes, *where the fire enters to inflame the charge;* as many persons who have had the misfortune to stand with their faces near the touch-hole of a musket, when it has been discharged, have found to their cost.

Now it appears to me to be extremely improbable, if not absolutely impossible, that a grain of gunpowder actually in the chamber of the piece, and completely surrounded by flame, should, by the action of that very flame, be blown out of it, without being at the same time set on fire. But if these grains of powder are *actually on fire* when they come out of the piece, and are afterwards found at a distance from it *unconsumed,* this is, in my opinion, a most decisive proof, not only that the combustion of gunpowder is by no means so rapid as it has generally been thought to be, but also (what will doubtless appear quite incredible), that if a grain of gunpowder, actually on fire, and burning with the utmost violence over the whole extent of its surface, be projected with *a very great velocity* into a cold atmosphere, the fire will be extinguished, and the remains of the grain will fall to the ground unchanged, and as inflammable as before.

This extraordinary fact was ascertained beyond all possibility of doubt by the following experiments. Having procured from a powder-mill in the neighbourhood of the city of Munich a quantity of gunpowder, all of the same mass, but formed into grains of very different sizes, some as small as the grains of the finest Battel powder, and the largest of them nearly as big as large pease, I placed a number of vertical screens of very thin paper, one behind another, at the distance of 12 inches from each other; and loading a common musket repeatedly with this powder, sometimes without, and sometimes with a wad, I fired it against the foremost screen, and observed the quantity and effects of the unconsumed grains of powder which impinged against it.

The screens were so contrived, by means of double frames united by hinges, that the paper could be changed with very little trouble, and it was actually changed after every experiment.

The distance from the muzzle of the gun to the first screen was not always the same; in some of the experiments it was only 8 feet, in others it was 10, and in some 12 feet.

The charge of powder was varied in a great number of different ways, but the most interesting experiments were made with one single large grain of powder, propelled by smaller and larger charges of very fine-grained powder.

These large grains never failed to reach the screen; and though they sometimes appeared to have been broken into several pieces, by the force of the explosion, yet they frequently reached the first screen entire; and sometimes passed through all the screens (five in number), without being broken.

When they were propelled by large charges, and consequently with great velocity, they were seldom on fire when they arrived at the first screen, which was evident not only from their not setting fire to the paper (which they sometimes did), but also from their being found sticking in a soft board, against which they struck, after having passed through all the five screens; or leaving visible marks of their having impinged against it, and being broken to pieces and dispersed by the blow. These pieces were often found lying on the ground; and from their forms and dimensions, as well as from other appearances, it was often quite evident that the little globe of powder had been on fire, and that its diameter had been diminished by the combustion, before the fire was put out on the globe being projected into the cold atmosphere. The holes made in the screen by the little globe in its passage through them, seemed also to indicate that its diameter had been diminished.

That these globes or large grains of powder were always set on fire by the combustion of the charge can hardly be doubted. This certainly happened in many of the experiments, for they arrived at the screens on fire, and set fire to the paper; and in the experiments in which they were projected with small velocities, they were often seen to pass through the air on fire; and when this was the case no vestige was to be found.

They sometimes passed, on fire, through several of the foremost screens without setting them on fire, and set fire to one or more of the hindmost, and then went on and impinged against the board, which was placed at the distance of 12 inches behind the last screen.

It is hardly necessary for me to observe, that all these experiments prove that the combustion of gunpowder is very far from being so instantaneous as has generally been imagined. I will just mention one experiment more, in which this was shown in a manner still more striking, and not less conclusive. A small piece of red-hot iron being dropped down into the chamber of a common horse pistol, and the pistol being elevated to an angle of about 45 degrees, upon dropping down into its barrel one of the small globes of powder (of the size of a pea), it took fire, and was projected into the atmosphere by the elastic fluid generated in its own combustion, leaving a very beautiful train of light behind it, and disappearing all at once, like a falling star.

This amusing experiment was repeated very often, and with globes of different sizes. When very small ones were used singly, they were commonly consumed entirely before they came out of the barrel of the pistol; but when several of them were used together, some, if not all of them were commonly projected into the atmosphere on fire.

I shall conclude this paper by some observations on the practical uses and improvements that may probably be derived from these discoveries, respecting the great expansive force of the fluid generated in the combustion of gunpowder.

As the *slowness* of the combustion of gunpowder is undoubt-edly the cause which has prevented its enormous and almost incredible force from being discovered, so it is evident, that the readiest way to increase its effects is to contrive matters so as to accelerate its inflammation and combustion. This may be done in various ways, but the most simple and most effectual manner of doing it would, in my opinion, be to set fire to the charge of powder by shooting (through a small opening) the flame of a smaller charge into the midst of it.

I contrived an instrument on this principle for firing can-non three or four years ago, and it was found on repeated trials to be useful, convenient in practice, and not liable to ac-cidents. It likewise supersedes the necessity of using priming, of vent tubes, port-fires, and matches; and on that account I imagined it might be of use in the British navy. Whether it has been found to be so or not I have not yet heard.

Another infallible method of increasing very considerably the effect of gunpowder in fire-arms of all sorts and dimen-sions, would be to cause the bullet to fit the bore exactly, or without windage, *in that part of the bore at least where the bullet rests on the charge :* for when the bullet does not com-pletely close the opening of the chamber, not only much of the elastic fluid generated in the first moment of the combustion of the charge escapes by the sides of the bullet, but, what is of still greater importance, a considerable part of the uncon-sumed powder is blown out of the chamber along with it, in a state of actual combustion, and getting before the bullet con-tinues to burn on as it passes through the whole length of the bore, by which the motion of the bullet is much impeded.

The loss of force which arises from this cause is, in some

cases, almost incredible; and it is by no means difficult to contrive matters so as to render it very apparent, and also to prevent it.

If a common horse pistol be fired with a loose ball, and so small a charge of powder that the ball shall not be able to penetrate a deal board so deep as to stick in it when fired against it from the distance of six feet; the same ball, discharged from the same pistol, with the same charge of powder, may be made to pass quite through one deal board, and bury itself in a second placed behind it, merely by preventing the loss of force which arises from what is called windage; as I have found more than once by actual experiment.

I have in my possession a musket, from which, with a common musket charge of powder, I fire two bullets at once with the same velocity that a single bullet is discharged from a musket on the common construction, with the same quantity of powder. And, what renders the experiment still more striking, the diameter of the bore of my musket is exactly the same as that of a common musket, except only in that part of it where it joins the chamber, in which part it is just so much contracted that the bullet which is next to the powder may stick fast in it. I ought to add, that though the bullets are of the common size, and are consequently considerably less in diameter than the bore, means are used which effectually prevent the loss of force by windage; and to this last circumstance it is doubtless owing, in a great measure, that the charge appears to exert so great a force in propelling the bullets.

That the conical form of the lower part of the bore, where it unites with the chamber, has a considerable share in producing this extraordinary effect, is however very certain, as I have found by experiments made with a view merely to ascertain that fact.

I will finish this paper by a computation, which will show that the force of the elastic fluid generated in the combustion of gunpowder, enormous as it is, may be satisfactorily accounted for upon the supposition that its force depends *solely* on the elasticity of watery vapour, or steam.

It has been shown by a variety of experiments made in England, and in other countries, and lately by a well conducted set of experiments made in France by M. DE BETANCOUR, and published in Paris under the auspices of the Royal Academy of Sciences, in the year 1790, that the elasticity of steam is doubled by every addition of temperature equal to 30 degrees of FAHRENHEIT's thermometer.

Supposing now a cavity of any dimensions (equal in capacity to 1 cubic inch, for instance) to be filled with gunpowder, and that on the combustion of the powder, and in consequence of it, this space is filled with steam (and I shall presently show that the water, existing in the powder *as water*, is abundantly sufficient for generating this steam); if we know the heat communicated to this steam in the combustion of powder, we can compute the elasticity it acquires by being so heated.

Now it is certain that the heat generated in the combustion of gunpowder cannot possibly be less than that of red-hot iron. It is probably much greater, but we will suppose it to be only equal to 1000 degrees of FAHRENHEIT's scale, or something less than iron visibly red-hot in daylight. This is about as much hotter than boiling linseed oil, as boiling linseed oil is hotter than boiling water.

As the elastic force of steam is just equal to the mean pressure of the atmosphere when its temperature is equal to that of boiling water, or to 212° of FAHRENHEIT's thermometer, and as its elasticity is doubled by every addition of temperature equal to 30 degrees of the same scale, with the heat of 212° + 30° = 242° its elasticity will be equal to the pressure of 2 atmospheres; at the temperature of 242° + 30° = 272° it will equal 4 atmospheres;

at 272° + 30° = 302° it will equal 8 atmospheres;
at 302° + 30° = 332°   ——   16   ——
at 332° + 30° = 362°   ——   32   ——
at 362° + 30° = 392°   ——   64   ——
at 392° + 30° = 422°   ——   128   ——
at 422° + 30° = 452°   ——   256   ——
at 452° + 30° = 482°   ——   512   ——
at 482° + 30° = 512°   ——   1024   ——
at 512° + 30° = 542°   ——   2048   ——
at 542° + 30° = 572°   ——   4096   ——

at 572° + 30° = 602°, (or 2 degrees above the heat of boiling linseed oil,) its elasticity will be equal to the pressure of 8192 atmospheres, or above *eight times* greater than the utmost force of the fluid generated in the combustion of gunpowder, according to Mr. ROBINS's computation. But the heat generated in the combustion of gunpowder is much greater than that of 602° of FAHRENHEIT's thermometer, consequently the elasticity of the steam generated from the water contained in the powder must of necessity be much greater than the pressure of 8192 atmospheres.

Following up our computations on the principles assumed, (and they are founded on the most incontrovertible experiments) we shall find that,

at the temperature
of   }   the elasticity will be equal to
                      the pressure of

$602° + 30° = 632°$ 16,384 atmospheres;

at $632° + 30° = 662°$ —   32,768   ——

at $662° + 30° = 692°$ —   65,536   ——

and at $692° + 30° = 722°$, the elasticity will be equal to the pressure of 131,072 atmospheres, which is 130 times greater than the elastic force assigned by Mr. Robins to the fluid generated in the combustion of gunpowder; and about *one sixth* part greater than my experiments indicated it to be.

But even here the heat is still much below that which is most undoubtedly generated in the combustion of gunpowder. The temperature which is indicated by 722° of Fahrenheit's scale, (which is only 122 degrees higher than that of boiling quicksilver, or boiling linseed oil,) falls short of the heat of iron which is visibly red-hot in daylight by 355 degrees: but the flame of gunpowder has been found to melt brass, when this metal, in very small particles, has been mixed with the powder; and it is well known that to melt brass a heat is required equal to that of 3807 degrees of Fahrenheit's scale; 2730 degrees above the heat of red-hot iron, or 3085 degrees higher than the temperature which gives to steam an elasticity equal to the pressure of 131072 atmospheres.

That the elasticity of steam would actually be increased by heat in the ratio here assumed, can hardly be doubted. It has absolutely been found to increase in this ratio in all the changes of temperature between the point of boiling water (I may even say of freezing water) and that of 280° of Fahrenheit's scale; and there does not appear to be any reason why the same law should not hold in higher temperatures.

A doubt might possibly arise with respect to the existence of a sufficient quantity of water in gunpowder, to fill the space in which the powder is fired, with steam, at the moment of the explosion; but this doubt may easily be removed.

The best gunpowder, such as was used in my experiments, is composed of 70 parts (in weight) of nitre, 18 parts of sulphur, and 16 parts of charcoal; hence 100 parts of this powder contain $67\frac{1}{10}$ parts of nitre, $17\frac{1}{10}$ parts of sulphur, and of charcoal $15\frac{4}{10}$ parts.

Mr. KIRWAN has shown that in 100 parts of nitre there are 7 parts of water of crystallization; consequently, in 100 parts of gunpowder, as it contains $67\frac{1}{10}$ parts of nitre, there must be $4\frac{711}{1000}$ parts of water.

Now as 1 cubic inch of gunpowder, when the powder is well shaken together, weighs exactly as much as 1 cubic inch of water at the temperature of 55° F. namely 253.175 grains Troy, a cubic inch of gunpowder in its driest state must contain at least $10\frac{927}{1000}$ grains of water; for it is 100 to 4.711, as 253.175 to 10.927. But besides the water of crystallization which exists in the nitre, there is always a considerable quantity of water in gunpowder, in that state in which it makes bodies *damp* or *moist*. Charcoal exposed to the air has been found to absorb nearly $\frac{1}{8}$ of its weight of water; and by experiments I have made on gunpowder, by ascertaining its loss of weight on being much dried, and its acquiring this lost weight again on being exposed to the air, I have reason to think that the power of the charcoal, which enters into the composition of gunpowder, to absorb water remains unimpaired, and that it actually retains as much water in that state, as it would retain were it not mixed with the nitre and the sulphur.

As there are $15\frac{4}{10}$ parts of charcoal in 100 parts of gunpowder, in 1 cubic inch of gunpowder ($= 253.175$ grains Troy,) there must be 38.989 grains of charcoal; and if we suppose $\frac{1}{8}$ of the apparent weight of this charcoal to be water, this will give 4.873 grains in weight for the water which exists in the form of *moisture* in 1 cubic inch of gunpowder.

That this estimation is not too high is evident from the following experiment. 1160 grains Troy of apparently dry gunpowder, taken from the middle of a cask, on being exposed 15 minutes in dry air, heated to the temperature of about 200°, was found to have lost 11 grains of its weight. This shews that each cubic inch of this gunpowder actually gave out $2\frac{4}{10}$ grains of water on being exposed to this heat; and there is no doubt but that at the end of the experiment it still retained much more water than it had parted with.

If now we compute the quantity of water which would be sufficient, when reduced to steam under the mean pressure of the atmosphere, to fill a space equal in capacity to 1 cubic inch, we shall find that either that contained in the nitre which enters into the composition of 1 cubic inch of gunpowder as *water of crystallization*, or even that small quantity which exists in the powder in the state of *moisture*, will be much more than sufficient for that purpose.

Though the density of steam has not been determined with that degree of precision that could be wished, yet it is quite certain that it cannot be less than 2000 times rarer than water, when both are at the temperature of 212°. Some have supposed it to be more than 10,000 times rarer than water, and experiments have been made which seem to render this opinion not improbable; but we will take its density at the highest possible estimation, and suppose it to be only 2000 times rarer than water. As 1 cubic inch of water weighs 253.175 grains, the water contained in 1 cubic inch of steam at the temperature of 212° will be $\frac{1}{2000}$ part of 253.175 grains, or 0.12659 of a grain.

But we have seen that 1 cubic inch of gunpowder contains 10.927 grains of water of crystallization, and 4.873 grains in a state of moisture. Consequently the quantity of water of crystallization in gunpowder is 86 times greater, and the quantity which exists in it in a state of *moisture* is 38 times greater, than that which would be required to form a quantity of steam sufficient to fill completely the space occupied by the powder.

Hence we may venture to conclude, that the quantity of water actually existing in gunpowder is much more than sufficient to generate all the steam that would be necessary to account for the force displayed in the combustion of gunpowder (supposing that force to depend solely on the action of steam), even though no water should be generated in the combustion of the gunpowder. It is even very probable that there is more of it than is wanted, and that the force of gunpowder would be still greater, could the quantity of water it contains be diminished.

From this computation it would appear, that the difficulty is not to account for the force actually exerted by fired gunpowder, but to explain the reason why it does not exert a much greater force. But I shall leave these investigations to those who have more leisure than I now have to prosecute them.

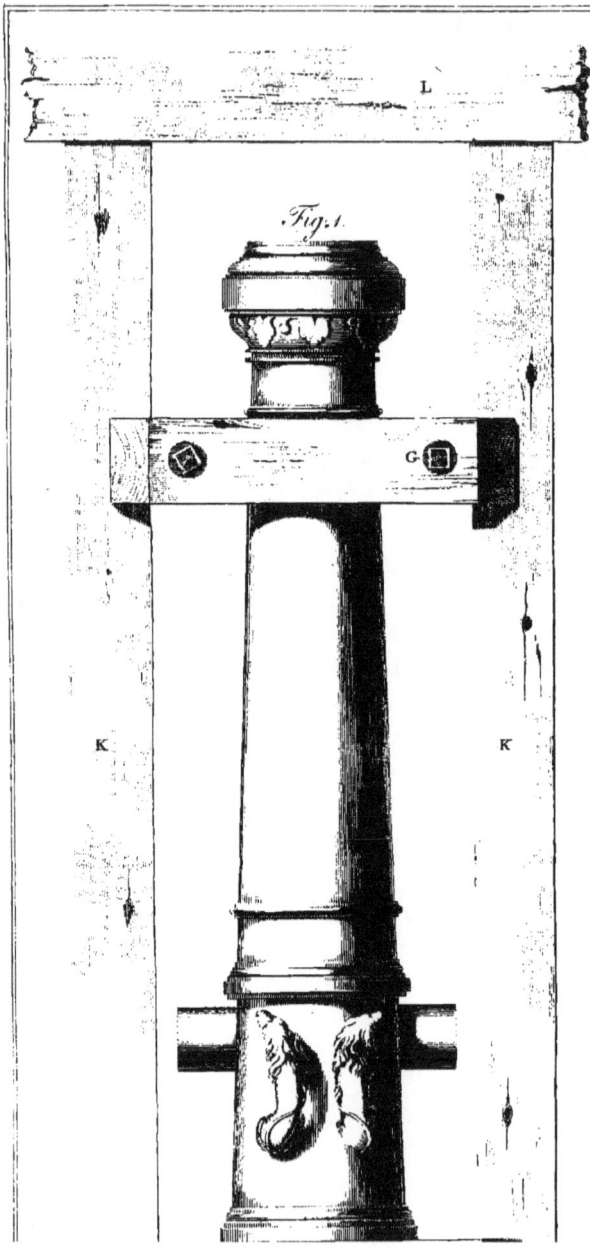

L

Fig.1.

G

K   K

Fig.9.

Fig.8.

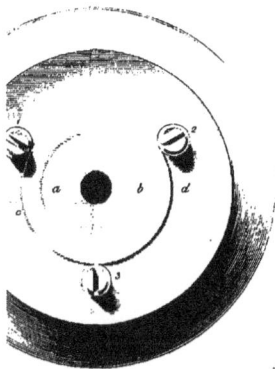

Fig. 5.

Fig. 10.

E

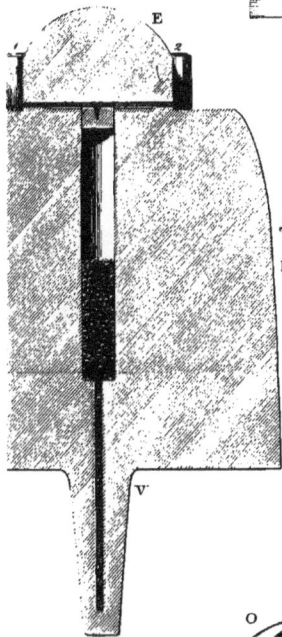

Fig. 2.

B

V

O   *Fig. 3.*

W

Fig.6.

Fig.7.

A

B

C

D

E

F

G

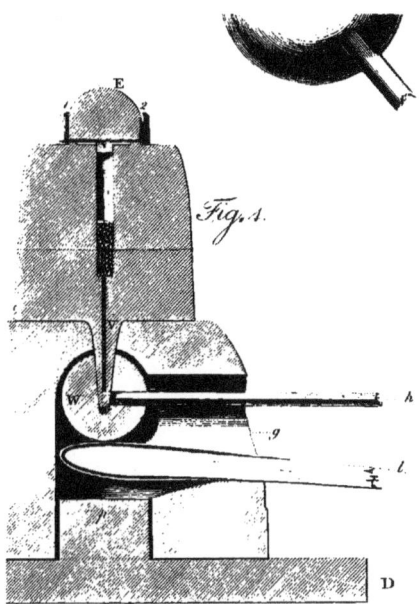

Fig. 1.

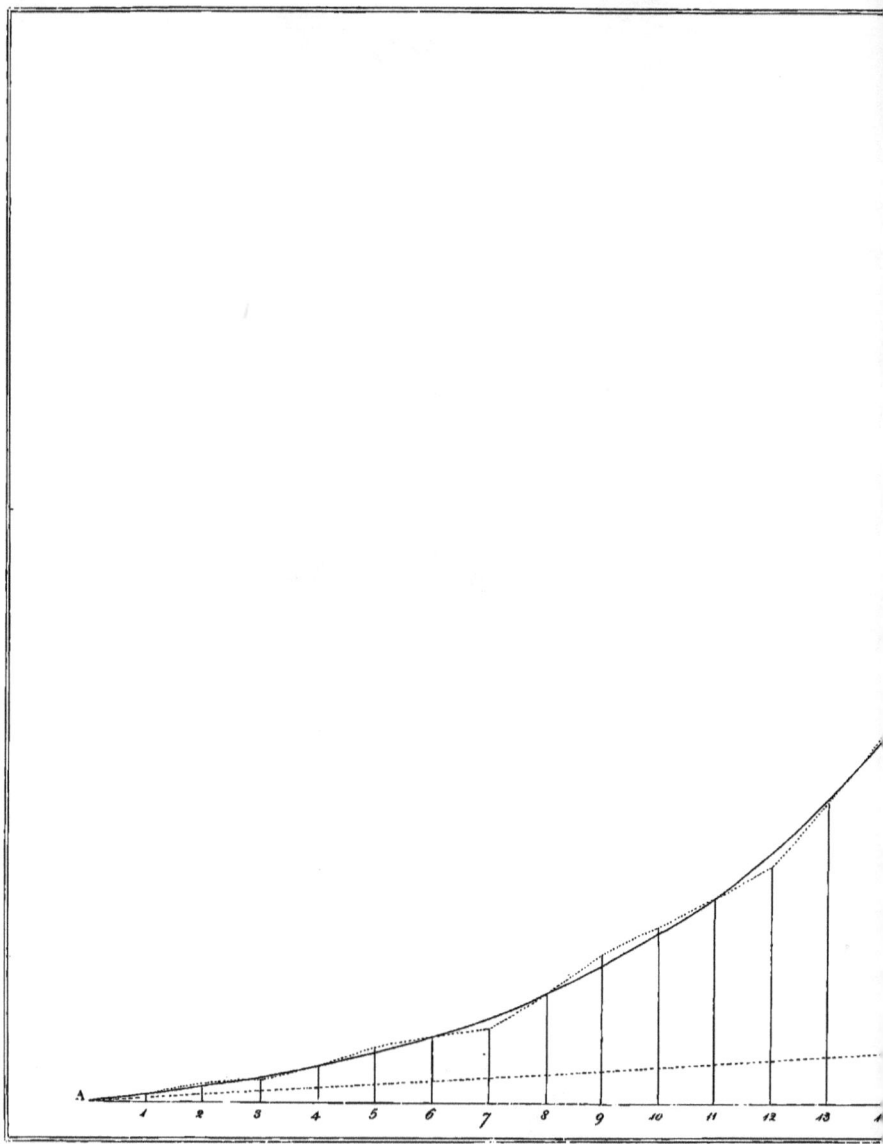

A   1   2   3   4   5   6   7   8   9   10   11   12   13

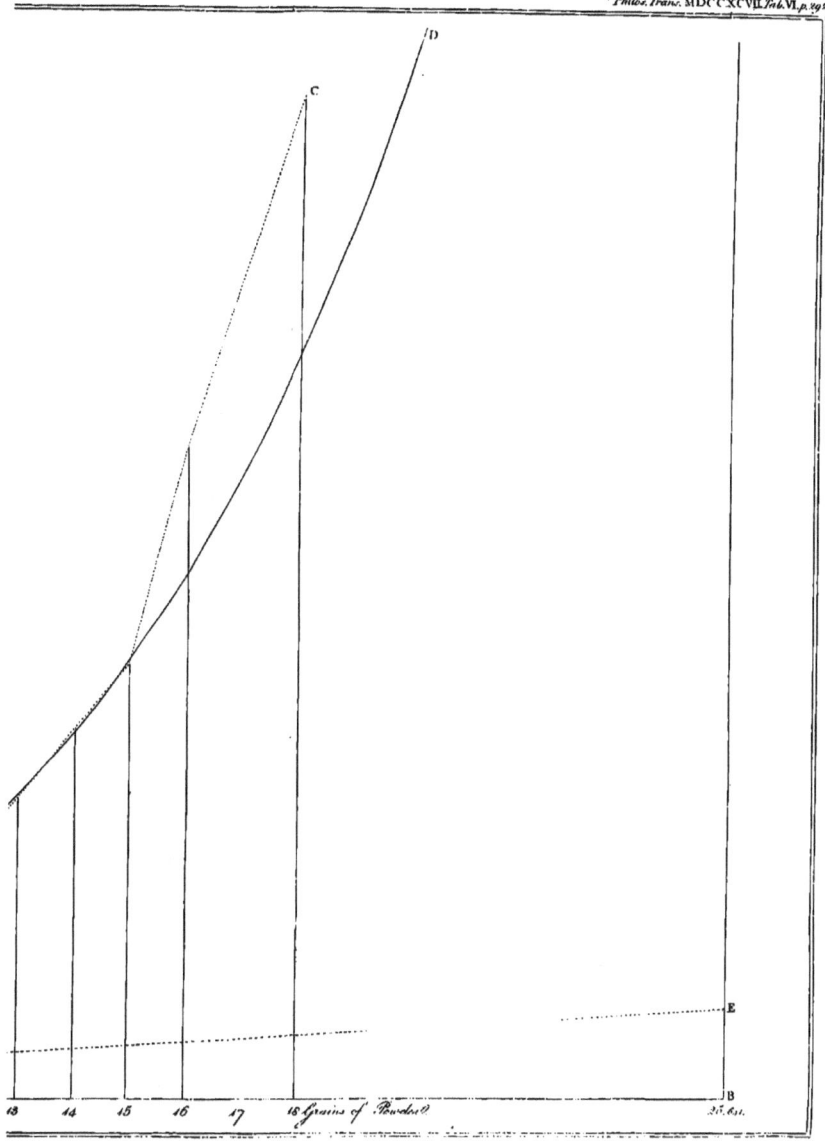

D

C

E

B

13   14   15   16   17   18 Grains of Powder   2 5. 651.

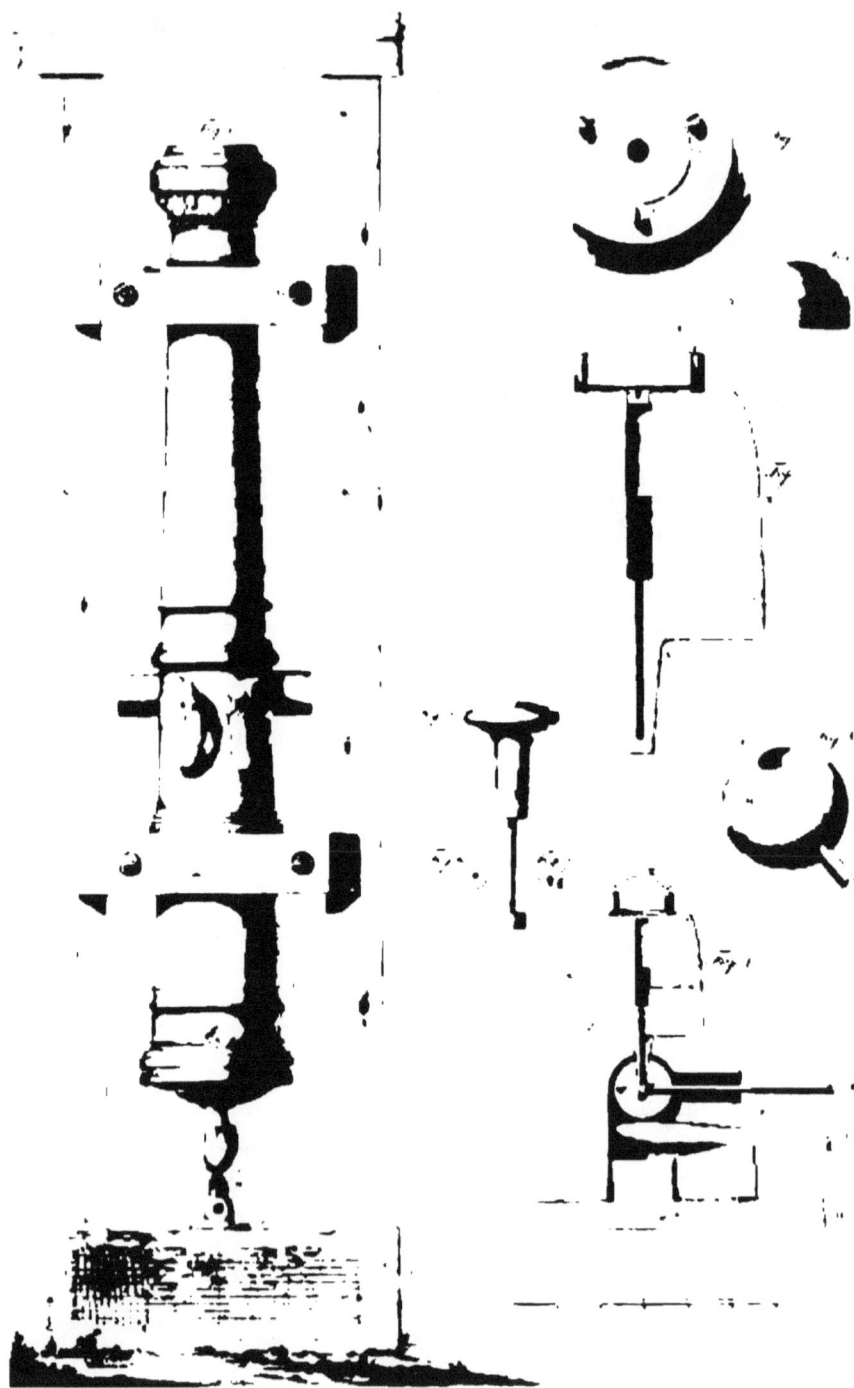

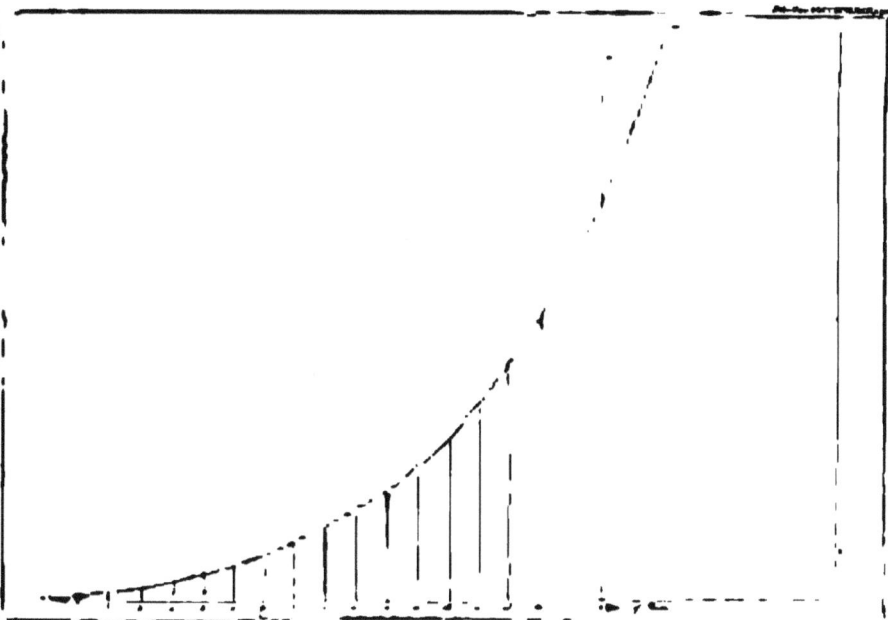